Alistair Shearer

The Hindu Vision

Forms of the Formless

with 165 illustrations, 15 in colour

Thames and Hudson

From the knowledge of Art arises divine knowledge,
and such knowledge leads to Enlightenment.
This liberation is truly the essence of the knowledge of Art.
He who realizes this, attains freedom.

VASTU SUTRA UPANISHAD

ART AND IMAGINATION

©1993 Thames and Hudson Ltd, London

British Library Cataloguing-in-Publication Data

A catalogue record for this book is available from the British Library

ISBN 0–500–81043–5

Printed and bound in Singapore

Contents

Forms of the Formless

The Hindu View of Life

As space pervades a jar both inside and out, so within and beyond this ever-changing universe, there exists one Universal Spirit.   SHIVA SAMHITA

To understand the premises of Hindu art, we have to jettison our modern insistence on the importance of the individual and the rational values of scientific materialism, and place ourselves back in the theocentric world-view of medieval Europe. In the Middle Ages the role of the artist was to portray and reinforce the shared symbolic order that had guided Western man since the advent of Christianity. This order derived from what was called the Great Chain of Being, a universal coherence which stabilized individual and collective life as part of a divinely ordained hierarchy linking humanity with God. In England this idea of a cosmic hierarchy, which persisted until well into the Victorian period, is expressed perhaps most clearly in the works of Shakespeare: when Macbeth murders King Duncan under his own roof, the act is a most unnatural deed not only because it violates the sacred duty of hospitality, but because in killing the hereditary head of state, he has violated the natural order that the institution of kingship both reflects and perpetuates. As a result of this violation of Cosmic Law, all sorts of unnatural things happen: storms blow up across the land, falcons are killed by owls, aristocratic horses tear each other to pieces. Until very recently, the preservation of the whole, with its apparent disregard for the pursuits of the individual, was particularly a feature of Hindu society, structured as it was by the reciprocal hierarchy of the caste system.

In Indian civilization, the operation of Cosmic Law is enshrined in what the West calls Hinduism and the Indians call *Sanatana Dharma* – 'the Eternal Law'. There is in fact no word in Indian languages to signify 'religion' as a discrete or separate social function. *Sanatana Dharma* is a complete way of life, regulating and governing the evolution of the individual from conception to death, life after reincarnating life, and to act in accord with the prescriptions of *Sanatana Dharma* is to live in accord with the law of Nature herself. The role of the artist in this vast scheme of things is thus not to redraw the parameters of possibility in perception or expression, or to criticize the inherited tradition or society, but rather to create those time-honoured forms which reiterate, glorify and perpetuate the Cosmic Law that upholds all life.

The levels of life

Most Westerners are baffled by the myriad apparent contradictions of Hinduism, which ranges with maddening ease from primitive cults of blood sacrifice to the most sophisticated systems of metaphysical speculation and mystical experience. This extraordinary variety of belief and practice is partly explicable by history. When the Aryan tribes, nomadic and imageless, entered India some time around 2000 BC, they found an indigenous settled culture – the Dravidians – that worshipped the Earth Mother in many forms and images and, at the most popular stratum, practised the irrepressible animism that persists even today throughout South and South East Asia, celebrating the continual epiphanies of nature – in rock, river, tree and snake.

The Aryans brought with them the Sanskrit language, reverence for the cow, and a complex body of sacrificial ritual. Their religious knowledge was encoded

Shiva Vishapaharana, the Destroyer of the Poison of Time. South India, 10th century.

5

in the *Vedas*, an oral tradition of chants which record mystical cognitions of the inmost structure and workings of the universe, and which have remained the backbone of *Sanatana Dharma*. As time progressed, a plurality of sects arose, each concentrating on one aspect of the Supreme, each with its rituals and mythologies. The resultant variety of belief and practice, though confusing to the Western mind, is not self-contradictory; rather, it is like the many facets of the one scintillating diamond. Indeed, it is this diversity that makes India the living museum of the human mind and has given its civilization such an extraordinary richness. Every striving of the human spirit has found its place in the spacious mansion of *Sanatana Dharma*.

The Many Gods, the One Source

Despite its incorrigible plurality, Hinduism is not as rampantly polytheistic as it appears. At its heart lies a vision of the universe as a seamless unity, the manifestation of a Supreme Consciousness. The most celebrated expression of this non-dualistic vision is the spiritual teaching known as *Advaita Vedanta*, systematized in the eighth century AD by the enlightened teacher Shankara, and it is from the perspective of *Vedanta* that all the theories of art and image-making derive.

According to *Vedanta*, the entire universe is alive, structured as an ever-changing field of vibrating energy that is the manifestation of the Supreme Consciousness known as *brahman* – 'the Unbounded'. All the myriad aspects of creation, the 'world of name and form' (*nama-rupa*), are nothing but the temporary and unbinding modifications of this Consciousness, from which they are generated, in which they inhere, by which they are all maintained as they pass through their changes, and into which they eventually disappear. As the source and essence of all phenomena, the Unbounded remains unaffected by its creations: 'Weapons cannot cut It, fire cannot burn It, water cannot wet It, nor wind dry It away' as the most popular text of *Sanatana Dharma*, the *Bhagavad Gita*, says.

This transcendental infinity of life, like the Godhead of Christian mysticism, is not directly accessible to worship, but its radiance is refracted through a series of ever denser levels in a continuum of vibration ranging from the transcendent through the subtle to the gross. As human beings we usually inhabit the grossest levels, only dimly aware of the possibilities that lie beyond the range of our senses as they normally operate. But our capacity to experience can be enormously expanded by various contemplative, physiological and affective disciplines – yoga, meditation, dietary regimens – for mind, like matter, is merely a point of particular density in the continuum of energy. The primary purpose of both religious and artistic endeavour is to refine and develop the mind's ability to perceive the subtle depths of life and ultimately the one Consciousness – *brahman* – in which all life inheres. Thus Hindu art is grounded in what the Indians call knowledge of reality (*vidya*) and the West would call mystical experience.

According to Hinduism, life is a continuing process of spiritual alchemy whereby the individual being, through countless incarnations, is gradually purified in the fire of experience to the point where he or she can consciously re-unite with *brahman*, the matrix of all life. The Sanskrit term used to describe creation and the journey of the soul is *lila*, 'the divine play', using the word in

Mandala of deity and humans.
Kashmir.

both its joyful and its dramatic senses. In truth, the universe is nothing more or less than the Divine playing an elaborate game of hide-and-seek with itself. For us humans too, the world is a stage, and each of us plays our brief, allotted part to the best of our ability. According to how well we learn the necessary lessons and pass the necessary tests of each incarnation, we proceed to the next life, the next role in the cosmic drama that unfolds through all eternity. And no matter how grim life may appear from the point of view of the isolated individual, whose present situation is the result of past actions (*karma*), from the perspective of the Divine it is always blissful. As the *Taittiriya Upanishad* exuberantly proclaims, 'From joy all beings are born; by joy all beings are sustained; and into joy all beings again return.' That this is the true nature of things will not be clear to us until we accomplish the purpose of incarnation in a human body, which is to transcend our customary limitations set by habit and ignorance, and realize our identity with the Divine from which all life springs. Artistic creation plays a crucial role in this process of discovery: the image provides, for both its creator and its worshipper, a means for the Divine to come to know itself again.

The realms of the gods

Sanatana Dharma, in harmony with ancient wisdom the world over, teaches that there are four interdependent areas of life: the gross, the subtle, the causal and the transcendent. The gross is based on the subtle, the subtle on the causal and the causal on the transcendent, which is the source of all. The deeper the level of life, the more potential it contains. Analogously, modern science tells us that matter is structured in interpenetrating layers – the molecular, atomic and sub-atomic – with increasing power at each level. Cultural life serves to bridge the gap between the relatively gross level of mankind, restricted within boundaries of time, space and causation, and the transcendent Divine, which is unbounded and eternally free. As the expression of the subtler and more refined levels, cultural activity is thus analogous to the intermediate world of fantasy that the child establishes between himself as an isolated body-ego and an increasingly distant mother. The subtle levels – the invisible realms that form the unconscious springs of our thoughts and actions – are the abode of the hidden energies, the unseen laws of nature that control, modulate and sustain our daily lives. It is the myriad aspects and operations of the Divine – the laws of nature through which it manifests the world of particulars – that are personified as the deities of the Hindu pantheon. At the causal level of life lie the basic forces of creation, preservation and transformation, personified by the principal deities Brahma, Vishnu and Shiva. A fourth major deity, the Goddess, combines the attributes of all three in her various forms. The subtle realms are personified in minor gods, goddesses and discarnate beings. On the macrocosmic level the deities embody the operations of the Cosmic will, conducting and sustaining the evolution of life. In the microcosm, holding court in the luminous caverns of the unconscious, they represent the myriad possibilities of the human personality, brilliantly dramatizing all the ways of being that are open to us.

The Sanskrit word for deity is *deva* – 'being of light'. Hindus acknowledge not only major and minor deities, each with its different forms and aspects, but numerous other intelligences: demigods, spirits, attendants, and a whole host of infernal and celestial creatures. They inhabit an infinitely fluid universe: each member of this huge retinue of subtle beings can interact with other members and the human world, just as in our daily lives events, thoughts and feelings weave often unsuspected or unnoticed patterns. Thus demons can win boons from the gods by prolonged worship and penance; humans can contact and utilize the strength of *devas*; elemental beings flit in and out of the human realm, taking whatever shape or form suits their fancy or their purposes. This elasticity of the imagination is a constant feature of the Hindu world-view.

'But are the deities *real*?' asks the rational mind. To which the answer is that there are any number of different 'realities' within the relative universe; only the unbounded Consciousness, in which they all inhere, is Reality. What is certain is that our normal, socially agreed reality as perceived by the gross senses is only a tiny fraction of what exists. As regards the sense of sight, for example, science tells us that greater sensitivity to the electromagnetic spectrum would give us X-ray vision into the world around us; infra-red vision would turn our environment into a warm cluster of shining lights; sensitivity to yet longer wavelengths would render our visual field as a field of television waves, and so on. In fact, beings in subtle bodies help or hinder us constantly, according to their nature. Just because we cannot see them does not mean that they do not exist.

'And are the deities projections of the mind or objectively outside us?' The answer is: both – it depends on our viewpoint. They are experienced as outside our individual ego – just as the outside world or our own unconscious is felt by the ego to be 'other' – but, as our consciousness expands, and we realize our true nature to be that unbounded Consciousness in which everything exists, they are apprehended to be within us, as is everything else in the universe. This vision of the world as it really is, in which the isolated sense of 'egoity' is seen to be a fiction fostered by countless generations of ignorance, is the perspective of Enlightenment. The *Ashtavakra Gita*, one of the seminal texts of *Advaita Vedanta*, describes this revolutionary perspective: 'The waves constituting the universe spontaneously arise and disappear in you, who are yourself the unbounded ocean of Consciousness. You suffer no loss or gain.'

The exploits of the subtle beings are not regarded as 'mythical' in the Western sense, i.e. unreal; or if they are, then we and everything else are equally unreal!

Head of the goddess Durga.
Orissa, 18th century.

To the Hindu, our distinction between myth and history, legend and fact, is arbitrary, for the outer world of 'reality' and the inner world of 'imagination' are equally real, continuously influencing and shaping each other, being mutually interdependent polarities in a unified field that is itself the dream of the Divine. In this field myth operates as the ancient archetype of possible behaviour, which is acted out in various permutations throughout all time; myth is the general and educative pattern of which history, both individual and collective, is a particular example. So within every myth lies a profound truth about life, hidden in what the Hindus call *sandhya bhasha*, 'the twilight language' that protects sacred knowledge from those untutored in its proper use.

The infinitely complex web of relationships that is the universe operates through a network of correspondences that connect each part of the whole and link the subtle to the gross levels. The system operates as a vast hologram, any individual part of which contains the image of the whole and is imbued with the energy of the whole. Thus each deity, itself an aspect of the universal Consciousness, is at the same time intimately associated with the world of particulars through its connection with a specific element (*bhuta*), sense (*indriya*), name (*nama*), form (*rupa*), sound (*mantra*), colour (*rasa*), diagrammatic representation (*yantra*), symbol (*linga*), and so on.

It is through these media that the deities, the causal energies of our world, manifest: they are the 'body' of beings that are themselves immaterial. In popular Hinduism the devotee chooses whichever aspect of the Supreme suits his or her psychological and emotional needs. Traditionally, a devout believer will worship three types of deity: the local deity (*gramadevata*), the family deity (*kuladevata*), and the personal deity (*ishtadevata*). On the most popular level, images are considered as magical presences with supernatural abilities, and as such radiate divine energy into the community. At a personal level, an image can serve to expand one's perspective, acting as a daily reminder either of the invisible celestial realms and one's own potential divinity, or, at the same time, of the essentially contingent nature of the world and one's own littleness.

To ignore the realm of the *devas* is foolish in the extreme; to do so is to act like the gardener who tries to tend a wilting plant while forgetting to water the roots on which its health depends. In any case, there is nothing we can think or do that does not depend on these laws of nature. The intelligent thing is to begin to work in harmony with them. This knowledge of dealing with the very roots of life is the prerogative of the priest (*brahmin*), who is the technician of the sacred, and it is from the sacred scriptures that the rules of proportion, style and correct treatment of the images derive.

Hindu Art and the West

As a man is, so he sees.   WILLIAM BLAKE

Despite, or perhaps because of, its exalted aims, there is something in the very nature of Hindu art which makes it impenetrable, bewildering, or even repugnant to the average Westerner. We are faced with a maze for which we lack an Ariadne's thread, an art inextricably embedded in a religious and cultural matrix which appears almost unbelievably complicated and alien.

This lack of receptivity is attributable to habits of mind that have taken millennia to mature. Aesthetically, we in the West are the heirs of the European Renaissance and a Classical standard of beauty based squarely on the human figure. To the Greeks the beauty and proportions of the human form enshrined more than just aesthetic value: Man was considered the 'measure of all things' and the perfection of the human body was believed to lead to moral, even godlike, perfection. Indeed, the cult of the male body achieved religious status, celebrated communally in such institutions as the Olympic games, which, forbidden to women even as spectators, was an initiatory test of young men that served the additional political function of expressing the unity of Greek civilization. However idealized the canon of beauty set by the Greeks may have been, it belonged squarely to the world of flesh and blood, faithfully recording the taut sinews of a daylight, human reality.

Hindu art, by contrast, is in no way anthropocentric. It celebrates not the perfectibility of man, but the already perfect realms of the gods; it eschews the clear certainties of daylight reality and floats in the shadowy enigmas of the dream; it pays homage not to the rationality of the world of the extroverted senses, but to the irrationality of an oneiric and invisible realm opened up by inward contemplation. Its figures are androgynously sensuous, celebrating a beauty not seen on earth.

Aesthetic differences are the expression of deeper cultural and religious ones. The European Renaissance attempted to combine the ideals of pagan humanism with the Judeo-Christian stress on human history as evidence of a covenant between a particular chosen people and their single personal God through his unique Son, their saviour. Hinduism, by contrast, deals in time-spans which are geological and astronomical rather than historical; the linear history of humanity, let alone one race, is held as nothing against the vastness of the cosmic cycles of manifestation and dissolution that occur time and again without end. And to limit the irruption of the Divine in human affairs to a unique historical figure would strike the Hindu as limited in the extreme.

In the progressive forging of our modern world-view, Judeo-Christian and Renaissance values were recast in the cold Northern light of Protestantism. Luther's Reformation drew on a distrust of the mystical experience already evinced in the Old Testament, where only Moses was allowed to have seen God face to face. Judaism abhorred the 'graven image', and the duty of the believer was to follow the teaching of the Prophets and obey the Law in the circumscribed realms of family, society and work. Thus the Reformation jettisoned priestly hierarchy, the 'impracticality' of contemplative life, the mystical use of ritual and images. Protestantism, the father of the modern world, is essentially a masculine world-view, dominated by the attributes of the left cerebral hemisphere, with its emphasis on rational and temporal perceptions and verbal and intellectual abilities. Our secularized world, endorsing the virtues of individualism, sobriety, hard work and scientific materialism, is the result. Behind this world-view lay the myth of unsullied objectivity, whereby Man stands apart from the mechanistic processes of Nature and She is there to do his bidding.

Hinduism and its art springs from a very different world view. Dominated by a bias to the right cerebral hemisphere, it is predominantly feminine, with its emphasis on the intuitive and the irrational, its flowing plasticity and disregard for fixed boundaries. Always strongly oriented around the group, family or

Woman with children. Orissa,
13th century.

caste, Indian society never created a scientific or technical revolution, remaining obstinately wedded to the sacred and the subjective. For all its abstract concerns, Hindu art never tires of celebrating the innocent, telluric power of animal and plant. 'Plants, oh you mothers, I salute you as goddesses' hymns the Yajur Veda; and just as our Earth, the Mother Goddess Prithivi – 'the widely-spread one' – is guiltless, so her creations are without sin, divine.

The richness of form and unregenerate sensuousness of Hindu art spring from a tropical sensibility that acknowledges the utterly invincible power of Nature and mocks our desire to order her creation. It is of the irrepressible fecundity of the jungle, rather than the austerity of the desert, that so much Hindu art reminds us. Its defined spaces surge with an exuberance of polytheistic form striving to emerge, like the bursting forth of vegetation after the monsoon rains. Swaying figures, their limbs smooth as sap-filled plant stems, writhe and twist in serpentine undulation; fantastic bodies sprout multiple heads and limbs like the unfolding of some exotic and lushly-petalled flower.

The *Shilpa Shastras* – the classical Hindu texts on the arts – emphasize a figure's unity with the surrounding matrix of organic life. Details mimic the universal forms of the animal and vegetal worlds, both considered more enduring, and thus ultimately more real, than the human realm. Faces should follow the perfect oval of an egg; eyebrows describe the curve of a drawn bow; eyes mimic the shapes of lotus petals or fish. The shoulders are modelled on the elephant, the trunk on the lion, and so on. To the Indian mind, man grows out of the elemental structure of the cosmos no more and no less than the plants and beasts. The universe is not subject to Man; Man is seen in the image of the universe. He is a participator, not a controller, ultimately as powerless as any other creature to resist the great organic tides of birth, growth, decay and death.

The effect of these cultural and aesthetic differences can be traced in the history of the West's reactions to Hindu art. The word that crops up most frequently in the early European descriptions of Hindu art is 'monstrous'. For Hindu art, with its many-limbed and hybrid figures, reminded Europe of the medieval visions of Hell, the Antichrist and the Apocalypse. Against this background, the Hindu gods in their baroque extravagance appeared to Christians as demonic creatures from a nightmarish realm where all natural boundaries had been transgressed and the light of the one true religion had yet to shine.

Until the late nineteenth century, relatively few people had actually been to India, and the popular imagination had been fed on a tradition of fantastic travellers' tales of the mysterious East in a tradition stretching back to the days of Pliny and Herodotus. Ludovico di Varthema, whose travels took him from his native Bologna to South India between 1503 and 1508, gives us the following description of an image of a fierce deity in a royal temple he visited in Calicut:

This chapel is two paces wide in each of the four sides, and three paces high, with doors covered with devils carved in relief. In the midst of this chapel there is a devil made of metal, placed in a seat also made of metal. The said devil has a crown made like that of the papal kingdom, with three crowns; it has also four horns and four teeth with a very large mouth, nose and most terrible eyes. The hands are made like those of a flesh-hook and the feet like those of a cock; so that he is a fearful object to behold. All the pictures around the said chapel are those of devils, and on each side of it there is a

Sathanas [i.e. Satan] seated in a seat, which seat is placed in a flame of fire, wherein are a great number of souls, of the length of half a finger and a finger of the hand. And the said Sathanas holds a soul in his mouth with the right hand and with the other seizes a soul by the waist.

Such lurid descriptions were commonly circulated and breathlessly repeated in travel accounts; the English gentleman traveller Sir Thomas Herbert was not unusual in repeating Varthema's description almost verbatim more than a hundred years later, and passing it off as his own. Other sixteenth-century travellers, such as the Portuguese botanist Garcia da Orta and the Florentine Andrea Corsali, reacted more positively; both were genuinely appreciative of the cave temple dedicated to Shiva on Elephanta Island off Bombay.

The first glimmerings of a more objective view began to emerge with the study of other cultures that accompanied the scientific revolution. In the eighteenth century, scholars re-examining the Classical heritage with a view to understanding the suppressed pagan traditions of antiquity found parallels between ancient Greek and Hindu myths which suggested India was not totally foreign to the Western psyche. Similarities between the great gods of ecstasy East and West – Shiva and Dionysos – and shared beliefs in the celebration of sexuality and the instinctive particularly intrigued the English theorist Richard Payne Knight, whose psychoanalytical approach, concerned with content rather than just aesthetics, was the first intelligent attempt to understand Hindu art on anything approaching its own terms. A small but intrepid band of Europeans began the vast task of studying Indian art: the French Sanskritist A. H. Anquetil-Duperron conducted a detailed and appreciative study of the caves at Ellora; the Danish natural historian and scientist Carsten Niebuhr alerted Europe to the Elephanta temple with his examination of its groundplan and sculptural panels; and a brilliant young member of the French Academy of Sciences, Le Gentil de La Galasière, produced accurate drawings of both iconography and temples that created much interest among European intellectuals, including Voltaire.

But as Britain's hold on India consolidated in the nineteenth century, Victorian art critics and scholars alike were almost unanimous in their hostility to Indian art. The vehemence of their denunciations reveals an extraordinary irrationality. A spokesman for the age was John Ruskin, who was genuinely convinced of the moral superiority of Christianity and of the material superiority of the West at its best. Grudgingly admitting that the 'Indians, and other semi-civilised nations, can colour better than we do' (Modern Painters, 1856), Ruskin concurred with a general agreement that India had produced a fine tradition of craftsmanship and decorative minor arts, an impression strengthened by the Indian displays at the Great Exhibition in 1851. But like other Victorian critics he felt that Hindu India lacked the moral fibre to aspire to 'high art', i.e. an art based on the empirical study of nature.

Ruskin attacked Hindu art because 'if it represents any living creature, it represents that living creature under some distorted and monstrous form. To all facts and forms of nature it wilfully opposes itself: it will not draw a man but an eight-armed monster; it will not draw a flower but only a spiral or a zig-zag.' The creators of such art, he concludes, 'lie bound in the dungeon of their own corruption, encompassed only by doleful phantoms, or by spectral vagrancy'. Such judgments were, unfortunately, the norm.

Durga slaying the buffalo demon.
Mysore, 13th century.

There were, of course, exceptions, individuals whose eyes and hearts were not closed through religious prejudice, chauvinism or fear of the unfamiliar. The Gothic Revival that Ruskin championed, which was responsible for revitalizing and intensifying the practice of Christianity in the nineteenth century, had a paradoxical consequence: with the new serious interest in medieval forms came an awareness that art, in the Middle Ages, was a form of devotion – and this led some thinkers to view Indian art in a more favourable light. Foremost among its champions were Henry Cole, George Birdwood and E. B. Havell. To their names should be added that of William Morris, who, as an outspoken critic of Victorian industrialism and economic imperialism, was also a vociferous supporter of both India's art and her villagers. It was Morris who, with a gift of a fine bronze of Hanuman, the Hindu monkey-god, inaugurated the collection of Indian bronzes in the Victoria and Albert Museum, which is still one of the greatest in the world.

Indian art fared little better for much of the twentieth century, when the prevailing orthodoxy was Modernism, an aesthetic which, following Mies van der Rohe's famous dictum that 'less is more', had no time for historical or symbolic references and non-functional form. Ornament, such a feature of Hindu art, was particularly taboo. In his essay 'Ornament and Crime' (1908), Adolf Loos, the Austrian pioneer of Modernism, castigated ornament as being suitable only for children, criminals or savages, being 'degenerate for modern man'. He declared that 'ornament is wasted labour.... It itself commits a crime by damaging men's health, the national economy and cultural development.' It is really only since the late 1960s, a time of psychic looseness and visual exuberance in the popular arts, that the sumptuous strangeness that typifies so much Hindu art has come to be one of an almost infinite range of tastes permissible in the free-floating plurality of the post-modern world.

But the message of Hindu art goes far deeper than mere fashion; it is the expression of a level of tranquillity that is almost unknown to the modern mind, chronically overstimulated by a plethora of advertisements, images and printed words, and generally unable to maintain a prolonged attention span. Hindu art demands a receptive quietness for its appreciation, for its images were created, and at their best can still evoke, a time of perceptual innocence when the pristine immediacy of form was still vibrant, and an image had the power to penetrate deep into the viewer's consciousness and effect a transformation there. Born in a society with relatively few sources of artificial visual stimulation, the art of Hinduism positively relishes the depiction of the dazzling richness of perceptual possibilities. It appeals both to the eye and the mind: unashamedly sensuous, it is also highly intellectual, conveying interlocking levels of esoteric meaning that rely heavily on a recondite vocabulary of symbols, allusions and word-plays. Simultaneously luscious and literary, it caters to both the people and their priests.

Sculpture

Part of the appeal of a Western Classical sculpture is that it represents a moment frozen in time. Our humanity, so noble yet so frail, is granted a poignant moment of immortality, as in a photograph: ars longa, vita brevis. Indian sculpture, by contrast, exists in the timelessness of Being, simply at rest within its own fullness, surrounded by silence. Even as dynamic a piece as the

Shiva as Lord of the Cosmic Dance. South India, 10th century.

Dancing Shiva is not caught in the moment of dance, as for example the Apollo Belvedere is caught in the moment of stretching out his arm, suspended for all time. With Shiva, dancing is shown as his elemental state. There is no history, no temporal boundary here: Shiva as the eternal Cosmic Energy is the creator of Time itself, yet while continuously dancing the universe, he remains somehow perfectly balanced: simultaneously still and active, ever transcendent to what he creates.

Moreover, much Western art since the Renaissance compels our attention in a way that presupposes there is a viewer there to appreciate its beauty. Like the Mona Lisa's teasing smile, it is directed at the viewer, aiming to engage his or her ego. An Indian piece, by contrast, is sublimely oblivious to the viewer. It has no need of our mortal gaze, and defies spatial boundaries by looking right through us, back to the rarefied celestial realm from which it comes and to which it rightly belongs.

If the Hindu work defies our striving for visual contact, it also frustrates our attempts to analyse. Just as a sentence can be parsed to unfold its full richness, so much Western classical sculpture is amenable to an interactive, linear analysis of its components that can gradually lead to an appreciation of the subject as a whole. But analysis of a Hindu sculpture will reveal only a list of its component particulars. The drapery does not follow the human pattern of ordering the personal appearance and emphasizing the natural structural elements of the body; the many attributes, weapons and objects in its hands, each with their symbolic meaning, do not contribute to the overall stylistic orchestration of the piece. They act instead – as with a medieval devotional image – as an abstract, secondary grid superimposed on the primary figure, the purpose of which is to lead the eye and mind to transcend the limits of the visual, concrete form. The visual progression afforded by the contrast of separately articulated elements, delineated by light and shadow, is not there in a Hindu piece; instead there is a holistic presence whose integral stability derives, as we shall see, from a type of 'subtle body' rather than the garb, limbs or ornaments. The result is a single and irreducible unit of Being, an 'all-at-one-ment' that demands and encourages a quiet receptivity in the eye and mind of the viewer.

Painting

The area of Indian art that pays most attention to the secular is painting, of which the fullest account is the *Vishnudharmottara* (c. seventh century AD). Yet even this text, having dealt with the theory of types, methods and ideals, then proceeds to explain how to make the correct forms of more than eighty deities, so as to be in actual contact with them and have them mingle in the world of men.

The different concerns of European and Indian painters can be seen in their respective attitudes to the 'objective' world. Subjects that have been fundamental to the evolution of European painting since the Renaissance were virtually ignored in India, which produced no genre of the secular female nude, and virtually no portraits or landscapes. What little portraiture there is, mainly of princely families, was derived from the traditions of Islamic and European invaders. Representation of landscape exists only in a very limited way, and there is no attempt to achieve either the topographical realism or the romantic depiction of the 'sublime' found in Europe. In fact, many miniatures approximate to the Western abstract rather than landscape tradition: their wonderfully sure blocks of colour, boldly juxtaposed, create a world of tonal relationships more pregnant with possible meanings than any figurative representation could be.

Landscapes in Hindu miniatures are symbolic rather than naturalistic, their constituent elements depicting the subjective mood or situation of the characters in the scene. Thus the cowgirl Radha, awaiting her lover Krishna in the forest grove, will sit under a sky heavy with oppressive rain clouds, which symbolize her suffocating sexual passion that longs for release. This connection between one's inner world and outer environment, expressing a subtle psychological truth, is one aspect of the primacy given to subjective consciousness in Indian culture. It was not, as European critics once thought, technical inability that prevented the Indian artist from representing the objective world: he chose not to. When he wished, he was perfectly able to depict nature realistically. Vegetation, and above all animals – carved in stone, wood or ivory, or painted in various media – are often depicted with a breathtaking tenderness that captures exactly the essential feeling-tone of the subject. This essence quality is called in Sanskrit *rasa*, and to portray the *rasa* is one of the prime duties of the artist, whether dancer, musician, painter or sculptor. The *Vishnudharmottara* mentions nine *rasas* as the nine basic feeling-tones: the erotic, comic, pathetic, furious, heroic, terrible, odious, marvellous, and peaceful. Each *rasa* elicits its appropriate emotional response (*bhava*) in the viewer: respectively love, mirth, sorrow, anger, energy, fear, disgust, astonishment and tranquillity. We have here a theory of aesthetics as moral education that Aristotle would immediately have understood.

In painting, each *rasa* had to be depicted in its appropriate colour. So too did the basic character of the subjects, which, according to the ancient classification of Vedic philosophy, corresponded to one of the three *gunas*, or ways of being that in various combination make up the world: spiritual (*sattva*), energetic (*rajas*) and dull (*tamas*). Put another way, each aspect of creation has, in varying proportions, the qualities of light, motion and mass.

Significantly, the word *rasa* is also used to mean both the sap of a plant and, in yoga, the inner current of bliss which activates all beings, even though it is habitually overlooked by the extroverted attention. Contrapuntally, the word most commonly used to describe the utter dispassion of Enlightenment is *vairagya*, which literally means 'colourless'.

Art as Sacrament

Works of art created by humans are an imitation of divine forms; by utilizing their rhythms, a restructuring of the vibrational rate of the limited human personality is effected.   AITAREYA BRAHMANA

According to traditional Indian belief every creature has its own purpose which it fulfils on earth. The purpose of the artist was to reproduce those Divine forms which in turn lead the spectator to union with the Divine. Exalted though his task was, there was no division between artist and craftsman in ancient India. The most usual word for art (*shilpa*) covered a huge range of creative and useful endeavour spread over all aspects of culture. *Shilpa* was divided into sixty-four branches which, in addition to the visual arts of painting, sculpture and architecture, included accomplishments ranging from dance, music and engineering to cooking, perfumery and making love. Art, in short, was the practice of all those refined skills that enrich our being in the world, bringing nourishment, fullness and delight to life. This delight was not just pleasure, which depends on the senses, but what is called in Sanskrit *ananda*, an inner, spiritual bliss that exists prior to, and independent of, any sensory or mental stimuli. This state of pure, unalloyed Being is the natural fruit of refining senses and mind by leading them away from the field of gross perception, through the subtle realms, to the unbounded level of life, which is our own nature. The attainment of this intrinsic bliss was not only the goal of artistic endeavour but also the highest spiritual experience and as such the affective aspect of Enlightenment. The great nineteenth-century saint Paramahansa Ramakrishna was once asked, 'Where do I find God?' His reply was, 'Look between two thoughts.'

The Sanskrit word *shilpin* cannot be adequately translated as 'artist', 'craftsman' or 'artisan' – though it includes all these meanings. To them would have to be added the concepts of 'priest' and 'magician' in order to convey the *shilpin*'s role and skill in facilitating a profound change in consciousness. All these meanings must be remembered here when, as we are forced to by our language, we use the word 'artist'. The role of the artist was to contact archetypal and transpersonal levels of reality, and to depict those levels in objective form. For both the artist and the viewer, contemplation of the divine form becomes a means of transcending the limited ego-personality into which we are habitually contracted and from which our suffering stems. The creative artist is thus an agent of liberation: he mimics the original creative act – the descent of Consciousness into matter – and the forms he creates facilitate the return ascent of matter into Consciousness. His access to the treasury of these alchemical forms is provided by deep meditative experience and a profound, ingrained knowledge of the traditional canon.

Generally speaking, Indian art is anonymous. The artist in traditional cultures, of which the Hindu is a prime example, is not particularly interested in individual innovation; he is not the isolated genius of the Western romantic tradition. He feels at one with the cosmic forces, an integrated part of his universe, not an alienated 'outsider' divorced from it. As an individual, such an artist does not consider himself fundamentally different from, or opposed to, society at large; he is a limb of the body, a cell of the organism, acting as a single entity yet inextricably part of an indivisible and organic whole. As such, he is embedded and nourished in a series of concentric matrices – family, social, cultural, natural, religious and cosmic – that enfold, sustain and strengthen his individual creative life. Stable in this identity, his role is faithfully to transmit those forms which preserve and continue the inherited structures and beliefs of his society; his brief is conservative not innovative, social as opposed to individual, educative rather than diverting. His concern is not to invent new forms, but to rekindle the vitality latent in the ancient ones. As the mediator of the sacred in daily life, his work is utilitarian rather than entertaining, and this is one reason why there is no division between craftsman and artist in traditional societies. The anonymity of the artist here is not the impersonal sterility of Modernism, but a transpersonal perspective and status. Personal idiosyncrasy was indeed expressed, in the loving detail of ornamentation that is such a feature of traditional art, but the free play of partiality was always subsumed into the greater organizing whole of the tradition. The artist wished to be remembered not so much as a unique individual, distinct from others, but as the most faithful transmitter of a transpersonal body of tradition, bequeathed to him by family and teacher. His immortality lay in the unifying connection to the source of the tradition, not in egotistical separation from it. Thus it was the work itself that was the testament which lasted through time.

We do know the names of some Indian artists from inscriptions. The builders and sculptors of the Hoyshala dynasty in South India left names in many of their ornate temples. In Rajasthan, history records the details of one family of architects who served the kings of Mewar over a period of no less than two hundred and fifty years. And in the south-west corner of that state, in the white marble Jain temples of Dilwara on Mount Abu, the sculptors Loyana and Kela even went so far as to be depicted on either side of Saraswati, the patron deity of artists, thus starting a trend with subsequent architect-sculptors in the area. But these are the exceptions. By and large the creators of even the most celebrated and beautiful pieces of Indian art remain tantalizingly unknown.

The Artist and Society

From the knowledge of Art arises divine knowledge, and such knowledge leads to Enlightenment.   VASTU SUTRA UPANISHAD

Hindu artists and craftsmen came from all classes of society, though the temple architects were usually *brahmins*, who served as priests in the buildings they erected. The knowledge of *shilpa* was an essentially oral tradition passed down, like all the other branches of Vedic knowledge, from master to disciple, father to son, elder to younger brother. But this exclusivity was not absolute: we know of instances where a particularly promising child was 'adopted' and educated in an artistic family.

In towns, artists were organized in guilds that operated under the leadership of a master craftsman. Each guild lived and practised in its own part of the city, with a temple housing the deity appropriate to that craft. Even today one can see remnants of this organization in the old quarters of cities like Varanasi and Jaipur. At village level where there would necessarily be less variety of creative occupation, the community itself took the place of the guild, and sometimes an entire village practised one craft, its menfolk travelling, if necessary, to the place of work and staying there for as long as the job demanded. Such itinerant labour patterns are still common in parts of India, especially among building labourers and musicians.

The material and physical means by which the artist's priestly skills were practised were provided by the patron. The majority of the patrons were *kshatriyas* – members of the warrior, or ruling, caste. The supreme patron, as in the West until relatively recently, was the king. The *Vishnudharmottara* (see above, p.14) is set down in the form of a dialogue between a sage and a royal patron, and historical records, patchy as they are in India, tell of some rulers who took an active interest in the perpetuation of *shilpa*. Mahendravarman, the

Chola king. Madras, 13th century.

seventh-century ruler of the mighty Pallava kingdom of South India, was the inspirer of his famous capital Mahabalipuram, just south of Madras, and was himself a 'tiger among painters'; King Bhoja, from Malwa in Rajasthan, wrote the *Samaranganasutradhara*, an influential eleventh-century compendium on the visual arts.

The bond between patron and artist was an intimate and reciprocal one. The patron was the prime recipient of the spiritual merit accrued by the creation of a work of art. In return for making possible something that was to uplift the general consciousness, his life was glorified by a benign influence that spread out in a series of unseen ripples to his family and to those under his charge. The *Shilpaprakasha*, an important eleventh- or twelfth-century text on temple building, tells us that a religious patron 'will always have peace, wealth, grain and sons'. For his part, the artist ensures the spiritual evolution of the patron whose interest commissioned the work in the first place.

In general, monetary payment was not made, though artists and craftsmen were relatively well-off and highly respected and there was no slave-labour. Payment was in kind: food, cattle, fine clothes, gold ornaments, and above all land; many artists were also cultivators. Once the artist was rewarded, his obligation ceased. He had earned his living and discharged his duty (*dharma*) by acting as the mediator for a divine form that would live on after him, magically to affect all who saw it, and he was again free, to enjoy an intrinsic lack of attachment that aligned him to the priest or the yogi.

The Living Image

The sculptor becomes the sculpture.   SOUTH INDIAN SAYING

The image itself is not the deity. It is a temporary form into which the divine energy can descend when correctly invoked, a vessel from which the nectar of sanctity can be imbibed. Rituals are thus an invitation: if pleased, the deity will respond. The time-tested rules of both ritual and proportion must be followed, because these are the ones that have been proved to be efficacious in representing and attracting the deity. Why therefore change them?

This accounts for the practice at annual festivals, when much time, effort and money may be spent fashioning an image, and yet as soon as the climax of the festival is over, the image is taken to the sea or the nearest river and ceremoniously thrown in. It has done its job in temporarily 'clothing' the deity; when the same festival comes around the next year, a new image will be made. Similarly, if an image is damaged, there will be no attempt to restore it, as it is no longer a fit receptacle for the divine.

Considerations of proportion, not aesthetics, determine the form of an image. As the *Shukranatisara*, an important iconographical text, states, an image is 'said to be lovely which is neither more nor less than the prescribed proportions'. The basic unit of measurement in any image is usually the length of the face. As well as overall size, the facial expression, gestures, posture, attributes, costume and colour are all laid down in the texts. Once the image is completed, it is purified and its eyes symbolically 'opened' in the crucial rite known as *prana pratishtha*, which breathes life energy (*prana*) into it. This consecration is indispensable, as it establishes the image's connection with the particular aspect of the Supreme it represents. The image is now open as a living channel for the transmission of divine power and blessing.

The locus of artistic creation was the temple or domestic altar. The temple was often carved, both inside and out, with members of the celestial pantheon and episodes from the myths. At its heart, each temple traditionally has a fixed image (*achala*) which always remains in the sanctum, and its replica or substitute, the 'moving image' (*chala*), which is taken out in procession at festival times. The latter were cast in various metals, principally bronze, as were the images intended for domestic worship. An amalgam of metals was sometimes used, the *pancha-loha*, or 'combination of five' – copper, silver, gold, brass and lead – being considered the most auspicious.

Communal processions are an important part of the Hindu calendar. They allow the devotee to make offerings directly to the image, and also, in times past, they permitted those low-caste members of the community who would normally have been forbidden entrance to the temple to make their own devotions to the divinity. Processional images are transported in a chariot (*ratha*) which serves as a mobile temple for the duration of the festival. Such *rathas* are often works of art themselves: huge wooden chariots covered with intricately carved panels of the gods and goddesses and topped with elaborate towered structures made of wood, bamboo and canvas and brilliantly decorated with cloth banners, flags, and often gold and silver tinsel.

The creative energy that inspired and sustained the temples, especially the large ones, was awesome. The records of a place like the mighty Brihadishvara Temple in Tanjore, South India, dedicated to Shiva and built around AD 1000, give us a vivid picture of the artistic life of a community whose main occupation was the maintenance of ritual worship of the deity. As well as the large images in bronze and gold, and the silver, gold, jewels and cash presented to the temple by the builder Rajaraja I, stone sculpture, painting and elegant calligraphic inscriptions were commissioned. Dance and music flourished, and each evening the community assembled for the worship of the deity and the chanting of hymns in Sanskrit and Tamil. Many thousands of acres around the temple were set aside for the cultivation of the rice, other foodstuffs, and flowers used in the daily rituals. Cooks, gardeners, flower-gatherers, garland-makers, musicians, drummers, dancers, jewellers, dance-masters, wood-carvers, sculptors, painters, poets, choir-groups, accountants, watchmen and numerous other servants and officials were all employed on a regular basis and, so the inscriptions tell us, given grants of land. Rajaraja constructed two long streets just to house the four hundred dancing girls attached to the temple.

As the major landowner and employer in the area, the temple was the centre of the community, the hub around which revolved the lives of rich and poor alike. Even today, remnants of this importance can be seen in the big temples of the South, which by and large have preserved their traditions more than those in the often-invaded North. At Shrirangam, over forty thousand people still live and work in the confines of the great Vishnu temple. And offerings can still be a sumptuous affair: at the annual festival at the great temple of Tirupati in Tamil Nadu, thirty-two types of flowers, weighing together 2,500 kilos (over 5,000 lbs), are offered to the image. It is within this vibrant social and religious setting that the images we see today, set somewhat forlornly in their museum cabinets, should be imagined.

Art, Ritual and Sacrifice

Know that all of Nature is but a magic theatre, that the great Mother is the master magician, and that this whole world is peopled by her many parts.
SHVETASHVATARA UPANISHAD

In harmony with cosmic rhythms, ancient societies dignified everything useful with ritual and sacred status; 'art' informed all aspects of daily life. Ritual ensures survival by ordering chaos into regular cyclic patterns of birth, growth, decay and death, thereby aligning us with the cosmic law of sacrifice. In this, repetition of the proven is more valued than novelty, and time-tested patterns govern the evolution of individual and society alike: ritual separation of the sexes, ritual observance of festivals, ritual rites of passage predicated on the rhythm of separation, initiation, apotheosis and return to the community.

The world of Vedic India was pre-eminently traditional: every action was understood to be part of the cosmic order and categorized and evaluated accordingly. The Vedic sages saw the universe as an eternal and colossal ritual of sacrifice, a 'making sacred' through relinquishing. For it is the self-sacrifice of the Absolute – the universal Consciousness personified as Purusha, the Cosmic Man – which, in a process of self-dismemberment, gives birth to the universe, the feminine Prakriti. Once created, the very nature of this universe is itself a ceaseless creation and letting go of form, a transmutation and recycling of energies, and every aspect of creation, divine and human, reflects this unending transformation.

We humans cannot live without taking part in this ritual, both as instrument and victim, and it is through our conscious recognition of this fact that cosmic order is maintained. The role of the Vedic priest was to perform sacrificial rituals (*yagyas*) which, as a symbolic participation in the true nature of life, upheld a harmony between its celestial and terrestrial levels. The earth is one vast sacrificial block, and from her very body were fashioned the bricks that build the Vedic altar. Just so, the altar is the earth in miniature.

Art and sacrifice are two reciprocal movements that together maintain life. Sacrifice surrenders forms into the formless matrix of Consciousness: symbols of creation – grain, clarified butter, milk, etc. – are offered to the purifying medium of fire, and dematerialized. This is the ascent of matter. Artistic ritual engenders forms from the formless matrix of Consciousness: subtle impulses of creation – gods, goddesses, images – are materialized through the solidifying medium of mind and senses. This is the descent of spirit.

Thus the disciplines of sacrifice and art have a mutually nourishing function, operating in complementary ways to re-establish the primary wholeness. As sacrifice is an art, so art is a sacrifice. Now the image is the altar, the fulcrum of conscious death and rebirth. The original creative act of Purusha's dismembering is repeated on a microcosmic scale as the individual artist, shaman-like, surrenders his limited and circumscribed sense of self into a silent openness from which he acts as a channel for the manifestation of perennial forms. It is his conscious emptying that allows those forms to emerge; once manifested, they in turn draw the viewer back to the silence from which they came, the fecund void of universal Consciousness.

The social integration of the artist fostered his integrity, nurturing a personality secure enough to transcend itself, an ego strong enough to die. This

Priest performing fire ritual.
Kangra school, 18th century.

process of self-transcendence (which is the characteristic of human maturity in general) was for the artist the specific means of creating. In short, the artist was like the priest: a specialized instrument of sacrifice through whose activity the community could align itself to that universal law of sacrifice by which all evolution is maintained, generation after generation.

Name, Form and Symbol

The imager, on the night before beginning his work and after ceremonial purification, is instructed to pray: 'O Thou Lord of all the Gods, teach me in dreams how to carry out the work I have in mind.'   AGNI PURANA

As space is the matrix of form, so silence is the mother of sound. According to the Vedic seers, all form is created in the apparent void of space, as all sound is generated from the apparent muteness of silence. It is from the silent void, the cosmic 'no-thing-ness' of unbounded Consciousness, beyond the grasp of the senses, that all creation comes.

The coherence of the sequential stages of unfolding natural law is crucial. These are cognized by the Vedic seer as sounds, which, in their precise detail and coherent sequence are codified as the *Veda*, and referred to as *shruti* ('that which is heard'), and they carry within them the structure of form, as the seed contains the tree. These packets of intelligence are encoded with the organizing power that structures the universe, and it is through them that creation is structured, maintained and dissolved, cycle after cycle.

In Vedic teaching, sound and form are inseparable. All the properties of the form are there in the sound, waiting to be structured on the grosser level as form. Conversely, all form is vibrating energy, movement, and movement produces sound. Thus every object and process in creation has its subtle constituent sound, and it is through the knowledge of these sounds – the science of *mantra* – that the world can be understood and organized.

Just as sound can unfurl the inmost petals of feeling and transport the mind to silence, so form can act as an instrument of transcendence by drawing the attention to the laws of nature that structure the universe. In this process, the symbol is crucial. For Hindus, as for other traditional peoples, art encodes the information that regulates social evolution in the DNA of sacred symbols. Such symbols are transmitted, not invented, by the mind of man; they are inherent in life itself, as the language of natural forms. Often synoptic, they carry many levels of abstract meaning in a concrete physical form, thereby bridging the gap between eternal values and temporal situations and structures.

The image is born deep in the consciousness of the artist, and as long as there is a connection with the nourishing source of tradition within, there is no shortage of images. But when for whatever reason this connection disappears, then men and women have only the superficial, gross world of form to turn to. All their cognitive power is used to penetrate and master the forces of nature for their own ends in the pursuit of greater material comfort. No longer rooted in their centre, their energy is dissociated from the world they are intrinsically part of, their awareness is dissipated centrifugally, and chaos results. A silver cord connecting the Absolute and the relative is broken, and a cancerous

Vishnu's conch-shell, signifying the primordial sound of the origin of existence. 16th century.

21

Varada mudra: Granting of boons.

Abhaya mudra: 'Fear not.'

Anjali mudra: 'I bow to the light within you.'

incoherence of the social organism sets in. In Yeats's words, 'Things fall apart; the centre cannot hold; mere anarchy is loosed upon the world.'

As the work of Jung and his followers has argued, the vocabulary of these archetypal symbols, our psychic DNA, is small but universal, unconsciously transmitted and appreciated, often surfacing only at times of crisis or intense need. The unifying, evolutionary function of the symbol is clear from the original meaning of the word, derived from the Greek verb *symballein*, 'to bring together'. Its synthetic nature makes the symbol fundamental to religion – from the Latin *religio*, 'I re-unite'. Indeed, symbolism is the key to understanding religion, which is itself the key to understanding life.

The fact that the form of the symbol is fixed by tradition does not mean that it is dead or inert. On the contrary, it is a vibrant living event, sprung fresh from the mulch of daily and psychic life. The form is repeated time and again but its meaning is experienced afresh each time. This process is reinforced by the periodic repetition of those communal symbolic acts – rituals, festivals, games – so loved by traditional and agricultural societies, who, with a childlike ability to experience anew, hunger not for novelty but for authenticity. For them art is not just recreation but re-creation, not a diversion but a re-membering through which the individual's links with community and cosmos are forged again and again, time after time. In this acknowledgment of individual transience lies, paradoxically, a supra-individual immortality as part of a greater whole – family, tribe or cosmos.

Though the form of a society may change, its need for symbols does not. The imagination of traditional societies, illiterate and rural, is excited by gods and goddesses; that of modernized town-dwellers by secular concepts of freedom, democracy and scientific progress. Both cases are examples of life striving to ennoble and nourish itself from its own fullness.

The modern, Westernized world can easily forget the symbolic nature of what it most values. Individually we all maintain our private rituals; collectively the need for ritual, and its attendant authority, has been largely transferred to the scientific method. For no less than art and religion, science is motivated by the desire to transcend the present limits of human knowledge and experience; all three utilize the repetition of what has previously been found to be revealing and rewarding. Religion and art repeat various externalized and internalized rituals of action and attention in seeking a deep psychic encounter with the unknown; science does likewise in seeking a deep conscious encounter with the unknown, even though its ritual is performed in the moral vacuum of the laboratory.

Symbols of Vishnu: his flaming sun disc; his feet as a *tilaka* mark worn on the devotee's forehead; his conch.

In social life, all forms of exchange are actually symbolic, for human activity is the interaction between those who take and store and those who give and spend. In any transaction – physical, emotional, economic, psychic – this dynamic of receiving and releasing is present in some proportion, for it is the basic pattern of the transmutation of energy which is life. In Hindu society, the reciprocal roles of patron and artist were just one of the variations on the basic theme of spiritual and worldly occupations, whose classic expression is the complementary duality of householder and recluse (*sannyasin*).

In its capacity to contain and celebrate ambiguity, the symbol illustrates the paradoxical nature of life in the mutual interdependence of opposites. This mutuality is alluded to by the repetition of the syllable *dva* (from which we get our word 'duality') in the Sanskrit word for 'opposite', *dvandva*. In the imaginative rhizome of human life, the symbol is an essential and fluid encapsulation of *karma*, the law of action and re-action which propels evolution. It is through symbols, the implicate patterning of activity, that the past – both collective and individual – is born in the present, and is in time transformed into the future.

The Act of Creation

All of me is on fire,
My voice, my body, my hands!
I tremble with the need to express.
Out of the earth I celebrate,
Out of the skies comes my answer.
Out of the earth I create his body,
Out of space his abode.
This bounty and this beauty is my source;
My body is the instrument of my expressions.
SOUTH INDIAN ARTISTS' SONG

The most important text for an understanding of the recondite reasoning behind the creation of a Hindu image is a little known-work called the *Vastu Sutra Upanishad* ('The Sacred Verses on Sculpture'). Appended to the *Atharva Veda*, this is the first text dealing with *shilpa* accorded the status of an *upanishad*, or divine revelation. Rather than discussing images in terms of the rules governing their proportion and the mechanics of their construction, as do the *Shilpa Shastras*, it deals primarily with the very principles of image formation: the cosmic origins of an image, its generation in consciousness, the material grounding of the image, and its ultimate significance. Thus in dealing with questions of a meaning that imbues yet transcends the physical limits of form, the *Vastu Sutra Upanishad* is a unique treatise on the pure, as much as the applied, science of iconography.

The text is presented in the form of a dialogue between the sage Pippalada and his three disciples, who are Vedic priests. It is predominantly concerned with sculpture, but all of the general and much of the particular material it covers applies to other media also. The text is composed of a hundred and thirty five gnomically succinct verses (*sutras*) divided into six chapters; each verse has an explanatory commentary. The most important for our purposes are Chapters 1, 2 and 4.

Celestial musician. Konarak, 13th century.

Chapter 1

Having begun by praising sculpture as a divine art, and the sculptor as an embodiment of Vishvakarman, the patron deity of art and craft, Pippalada goes on to define a sculptor (*sthapaka*).

Sutra 4: *He who has the knowledge of circle and line is a* sthapaka.

Commentary: Holding in one hand a measuring rod of *khadira* wood and a cord of *darbha* grass fitted with a ring, that is his outer aspect. This knowledge is the knowledge of Art. From the knowledge of Art arises divine knowledge, and such knowledge leads to liberation. This liberation is truly the essence of the knowledge of Art. He who realizes this, attains.

On the gross level Pippalada's meaning is obvious: a sculptor is the person with the technical skill to use the compass and measuring devices by which the image is first located in the stone. But the circle and line interact, on a subtle level, as abstract structural elements; apparently opposed, the two forms are complementary. The circle exemplifies the feminine principle: it contains, by shepherding towards a centre, it creates volume and mass, it limits and is essentially circumscribed, static. The line exemplifies the masculine principle: itself uncreative until checked, but dynamic, unfettered, penetrating, divisive, running into space, unlimited. From these two all other forms – plane, cube, sphere, triangle, etc. – are born.

The symbolism of line and circle operates on yet another level: the consciousness of the sculptor. Vedic texts speak of Enlightenment as a consciousness state in which the mind is able to focus on the localized boundaries of the world while simultaneously retaining an awareness of the unbounded Consciousness which is our true Self and in which the world inheres. The *Bhagavad Gita* describes this enlightened perspective: 'He whose self is established in yoga, whose vision everywhere is even, sees the Self in all beings and all beings in the Self.'

Sanskrit refers to two ways of seeing (root *pash*), differentiated by their respective prefixes: *vi-pash*, 'seeing separation', is perceiving the boundaries in an analytic way, in a 'line vision'; and *sam-pash*, 'seeing together', is synthesizing the component parts into a greater whole, in a 'circle vision'. In terms of our perceptual apparatus this dual perception is located in the complementary functioning of the two cerebral hemispheres: the left concerned with analytical and rational perception, the right with intuitive and synthesizing ability. Normally the hemispheres are random and unsynchronized in their neurological activity; it is only in the state of meditation that they function coherently together. Psychologically, a simultaneous awareness of the whole and the parts, the figure and the background, is a symptom of integration, impartiality and equanimity, a balancing of the masculine and feminine ways of being in the world. Iconographically, this balance is symbolized in the union of Shiva and Parvati as the hermaphrodite Ardhanarishvara, 'the Lord who is half-woman'.

In Sutra 8, Pippalada enumerates the six essentials that the stone carver must master. These are:
1 the knowledge of stones
2 the compositional diagram
3 the carving and dressing of stone
4 the arrangement of the various elements of a sculpture
5 the representation of the essential mood-character of a piece
6 the final integration of all its component parts.

The ideal image-maker is thus both yogi and priest. As a yogi, he experiences the unboundedness of Consciousness, realizing that he is, in fact, the silent witness of all activity, in truth 'neither acting nor causing action to be done' (*Bhagavad Gita*). At the same time he is like the Vedic priest, through whose ritualized activity and precise expertise are fashioned those forms by which others can aspire to the same realization of wholeness.

Chapter 2

The image begins with a circle. Just as the form of the deity has arisen in the silent mind of the sculptor, so the image of the god will appear from the emptiness of the circle. Once the circle is drawn, the next step is to divide it into the *khila-panjara* (khila = 'emptiness', *panjara* = 'skeleton') — a compositional diagram, sketched out on the stone with finely ground powder, which serves as the bare bones of a composition around which the body of the image grows.

Pippalada then describes the drawing of a circle on the stone, and its subdivision by means of lines, as being the first steps in a creative process which is a microcosmic re-enacting of the universal creative impulse.

Sutra 6: *First, a circle.*

Commentary: The circle is the All, the universe.... The breath of life is contained in its form, even as the mind is in man. The circle consists of its centre and its boundary.... The support of the circle is the immortal, central point [*bindu* = 'seed'] in its firm position, stable like the pure consciousness behind the mind...

Sutra 7: *By the connection of one with one a unity is formed.*

Commentary: The circle truly is the Wholeness, of which the *bindu* is the support. . . . Just as all living beings evolve in it, so the many forms originate. That is the breath of life. This unified field has to be divided to obtain the limbs, or parts, of the image.

This division of the circle evokes both the creation and the composition of the universe. First it is divided in two by a vertical line, and then into four by a horizontal. The two lines symbolize respectively the elements of fire (masculine) and water (feminine), while the resulting four areas are likened to the four corners of the universe and the four cardinal directions.

Sutra 8: *All limbs have to be set along the lines.*

Commentary: . . . The line is the support of the composition, it is like a boundary. It is that which corresponds to the elements and to the gods in the unfoldment of action.

Sutra 9: *Straight lines are as rays of light.*

Commentary: By the line the sculptors divide the circle, as the creators by their action divide the world. From these lines in this way all the parts of the image manifest themselves visibly for the sake of the whole image . . .

From these intersecting lines a square or rhombus is formed, and the diagonals, representing the winds and the mid-points, are added (*Fig. 1*).

The reference to 'lines of light' conjures an image of the brilliance of a scintillating crystal or a hologram rather than opaque stone. This is apposite: to the enlightened eye the supposedly solid physical world is seen as a radiant dance of varying gradations of energy and light, a perception caught in the Sanskrit word most commonly used for 'image' – *murti* – which literally means 'crystallization'. In truth space is not empty, but alive with a network of energy lines, which, like some spider's web of subtle filaments of consciousness, continuously vitalize the manifested world, and silently direct the shape of gross form.

One result of the interrelatedness of all life is that no-one stands at a point in space that is isolated and meaningless; on the contrary, each point in the scintillating unified field of Consciousness is subtly linked, and each reflects the others. It is possible not only to conceive but actually to experience the universe, both physical and psychic, as this unified field without obstructions, a field of infinite correlation in which each apparently solid form is like a piece of crystal whose luminosity depends on the reflection of the luminosity of all the other crystals in the field. When viewed in this unrestricted way, with each being a temporary crystallization of Consciousness, reality is experienced as what the Vedantic texts call 'Indra's Net of Jewels'. According to the enlightened perspective, we are not the isolated atomic ego we seem to be, a solid 'self' defined by bodily limits and contracted over and against the 'outside world'. On the contrary, each being enjoys its own consistency only by virtue of connections that simultaneously compose other beings in the field. In this way the abstract whole is given character and focus by its manifested individual parts, while the parts, evanescent in themselves, are granted stability, dignity and ultimately divinity by virtue of their intimate relationship to the whole.

This view of all life, from the individual to the sub-atomic particle, as a fluctuating energy pattern, webbed into all other energy patterns, including

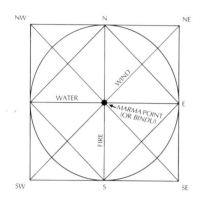

Fig. 1: Khila-panjara.

non-physical states, resonates more with some of the most advanced theories of quantum physics than with the 'classical' view of reality inherited from Descartes and Newton. It also accounts for the miraculous fluidity which characterizes Hindu divine and enlightened beings, whose behaviour defies all common-sense or mundane limits of time and space.

The *khila-panjara* diagram must be correct to ensure the structural and functional efficacy of the image. In its other meaning of 'cage', the word *panjara* aptly evokes the limitation, framed by human artifice, by which Universal Consciousness — essentially free, attributeless and unbounded — is held and structured into an individual form on the material plane. In this sense, the artist's compositional 'cage' is an analogue of his own body: a temporary localization of That which can hardly be localized.

From the *khila-panjara* certain seed-forms can be drawn. The triangle, called, significantly, *trihuta* ('the three sacrificial offerings'), unites the essential concepts of verticality, fire and humanity. Verticality is the distinguishing characteristic of the human species, distinguishing us from the other animals and symbolizing our eternal aspirations. The vertical is simultaneously the *axis mundi* around which the universe revolves and the link between earth and heaven, mankind and gods. As such it is represented in Hindu art by many interconnected archetypal forms: Purusha, the Cosmic Man; Mount Meru, the central axis of the universe; the sacred tree in all its variegated forms; the lingam, supreme symbol of Shiva; the upright human being; the sacrificial post (*yupa*); the ascending tongues of flame that consume the ritual sacrifice.

If the vertical direction symbolizes humanity *per se*, the human as creator is symbolized by the element of fire. Man is born from fire: generated by the ardour of desire and 'cooked' in the womb. Mastery of fire sparked the beginnings of settledness and civilization. As the centre of the home, fire transforms the raw into the cooked; as *agni* it is the digestive power by which man lives; as the skill of Vishvakarman, 'The Maker of All', it is the mother of technology. Psychologically, fire is the burning desire which impels all action, the insight which purifies ignorance and kindles illumination, the very light (*tejas*) of intelligence. Spiritually, fire is both the nourishing heart of the Vedic social religion, and the austerity (*tapas* = 'heat') of the meditative ascetic who dwells far from the domestic hearth. And as the element which corresponds with the sense of sight, fire plays an important part in Indian theories of colour, being seen as the vitalizing force in chromatic brilliance. The *Chandogya Upanishad* tells us: 'The essential redness of fire, that is the form of light; the essential whiteness of fire, that is the form of water; the essential darkness of fire, that is the form of earth. The intrinsic nature of fire then withdraws. . . . What is left are the three forms.'

From the triangle comes the hexagram (*satkona* = 'six angles'), an archetypal form that well symbolizes the reciprocal processes of creation and sacrifice at the very heart of life (*Fig. 2*). It is the interlocking of two triangles: the upward, representing fire and the masculine principle, Shiva and the phallic *lingam*; and the downward, signifying water and the feminine principle, *shakti* and the *yoni* (womb or vagina). In Vedic thought it is from the union of the two apparently irreconcilable opposites of fire and water that creation, the 'Great Delight', arises, and it is by their interaction that it is ceaselessly vitalized and maintained. This symbol is technically known as 'the symbol of the attraction of opposites' (*akarshani-yantra*). Sutra 17 of the same chapter alludes to its potency in

Fig. 2: Satkona.

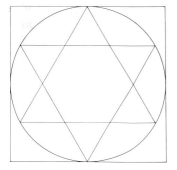

summoning divine energies when it says: '*The hexagram is the special sign of attraction*'; the commentary adds that the hexagram not only wards off negative influences but 'is the best means for revealing the character of the deity'.

Chapter 4

The next practical step in the creation of an image is to draw on the stone a grid (*koshthaka*) which complements but does not obstruct the existing *khila-panjara*.

Sutras 4–8: *According to the knowledge of the principles, for making images a grid is most important. Making squares is the principal work. One should visualize the various parts of the image within the grid. The essential feeling tone of the image arises from the measured gestures of its limbs. If the image transgresses the grid it becomes faulty.*

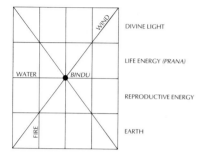

Fig. 3: *Koshthaka.*

The grid is described in full elsewhere (at the beginning of Chapter 6) as being a matrix of five lines by five, making sixteen identical squares or rectangles intersected by two diagonals (*Fig. 3*). This recalls the original creation of the universe, when Purusha, the Cosmic Man, sacrificed himself into 'sixteen parts', including the elements and the cardinal directions. 'Purusha has sixteen parts' says the *Shatapatha Brahmana*. Each type of line symbolizes an element as before: vertical lines are fire, horizontal are water, and diagonal are wind. To complete the symbolic picture, the bottom row of four squares, 'from foot to knee', represents earth; the next, 'from knee to navel', symbolizes reproductive energy; the third, 'from navel to neck', is the area of the life-breath; and the top, 'from neck to crown', is the area of the divine light.

The grid is then divided into five fields (*Fig. 4*), each field corresponding to one of the five hierarchical realms of the universe, which, in descending order, are 'the realms of brahman, *of the gods, of secondary divinities, of living beings, and of worshippers*' (Sutra 9). Into this grid will be projected the image of the deity and its accompanying figures (*Fig. 5*). Conversely, any sculptural panel can be analysed in terms of this subdivision into fields, which are superimposed on a basic structure of radiations from the central point of an encompassing circle (*Fig. 6*).

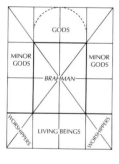

Fig. 4: *Fields of the koshthaka.*

Fig. 5: *Deity and attendant figures.*

Fig. 6: *Sculptural panel based on compositional grid.*

This creative central point of the grid, the 'immortal navel' of the *bindu*, is also found at the heart of Hindu architectural groundplans, both religious and secular. It *'is to be considered as the unbounded* brahman' (Sutra 8), and is also called the *marma*, and *'this centre is the life-breath of the earth'* (Sutra 14). In other words, it is the node point where intelligence activates matter.

Exactly the same mechanism occurs in the microcosm of the human nervous system. Ayurveda, the ancient Indian medical science, speaks of the 107 *marma* points in the subtle nervous system, of which the three most important are the three prime junction-points between cosmic intelligence and human physiology. These are in the lower pelvic region (governing bodily functions), the solar plexus (governing feelings), and the head (governing intelligence). In yoga they are known, respectively, as the 'knots' (*granthi*) of Shiva, Vishnu and Brahma. In the depiction of the image, two *marma* points are marked, the solar plexus and the head; the lowest one is irrelevant to a deity, as a discarnate being.

The structuring of a linear framework to lure the formless Absolute into relative form is the sculptor's (and builder's) equivalent of the priest's tracing out the groundplan for the Vedic sacrificial altar; indeed 'there is no essential difference', as the commentary to Sutra 10 tells us. Accordingly, each step in the creation of an image was considered a sacrificial offering and was accompanied by appropriate mantras. First the propitious moment for beginning the work was determined by the astrologer, then the selected stone was set on sacred *darbha* grass, polished and purified with milk from a cow of a particular yellow colour which represented *shakti*, the creative feminine power. Other materials received no less respect: the carpenter would ask the permission of the spirits residing in a tree before felling it, and anoint his axe with honey and clarified butter to soften the blow. After the sculptor had taken a ritual bath, meditated, and saluted his teacher, he made offerings – flowers, incense, unhusked rice, a broken coconut – to the line of teachers and the very tools he was about to use. Only then did he take the measuring thread, establish the central *marma* point and begin to trace out the circle and the lines. Before the chisel touched the stone, it was sharpened by being dipped in sacred cow urine, smeared with oil and whetted on leather, and the goddess of the chisels was invoked and mentally or verbally saluted, so as to bless the tools and process of carving. During the carving, sculptors wore ritually blessed amulets to ward off accidents. So highly was the material valued that even the chips of stone freed by the chisel were collected up and ceremoniously cast away with the correct mantras, just as one would dispose of the remnants of a sacrificial offering. Even today, many Indian craftsmen consecrate their tools at the autumnal festival of Dusshera, on the day especially sacred to Vishvakarman, their tutelary deity.

Contemplation, Worship and Transcendence

The man who never travelled to heaven in his thoughts and mind is no artist.   WILLIAM BLAKE

Whatever the status of the *devas*, and the effects these subtle beings work in the manifest world, there is in addition another level of understanding, to which the texts constantly allude, which is an inner one, related to meditation. An esoteric text, the *Mahanirvana Tantra*, tells us: 'The highest state is that in which the

Unbounded Consciousness is perceived in everything. Lower than that is meditation. Lower than that is the singing of devotional songs; lowest of all is external worship.'

The realization of this 'highest state' is the ultimate goal of Indian spiritual endeavour, whether religious, artistic, or philosophical. According to *Vedanta*, the philosophical system that encapsulates the highest Vedic teachings, the subject, the object and the process of perceiving that unites the two are all, in truth, the One undivided Consciousness, playfully unfolding itself in its threefold aspect of seer, seen, and the process of seeing. Enlightenment is the realization that we are and always have been only this unified field of Consciousness, immortal and eternally free, in which the individual perceiving ego and the perceived 'outside world' both inhere. The radically altered perspective of Enlightenment challenges all our habitual and cherished assumptions about ourselves and our life. It flies in the face of our most tenaciously held mis-perception – known in Sanskrit as *pragya parad*, 'the mistake of the intellect' – which is our erroneous identification with the limited and individual ego-sense. This mistake, fostered and compounded by all the usual processes of education and society, is the source of ignorance and suffering. To overcome this fundamental error, the ego has to be gradually led to a re-cognition of the original unity by a reversal of the usual mechanics of perception.

The means rest in the very nature of life itself. Just as matter contains within itself different strata of energy not normally evident – atomic, sub-atomic and beyond – so every object has subtler, inner levels not normally perceptible to our senses in their normal unrefined way of functioning. The technique is to select an object of one of the senses as the focus of attention, and begin to appreciate its finer values. As this happens, the perceiving mind will become correspondingly refined; the two go together. Eventually the finest level of the object will be experienced, and correspondingly, the most refined level of mental activity is attained. When even this movement of the mind is transcended, mental activity comes to a complete standstill. The mind thus ceases to be an individual ego-entity and falls back into its source, the universal Consciousness, as a wave falls back into the sea.

While the 'external worship' that the *Mahanirvana Tantra* sets as the lowest form of spiritual exercise is, like religion the world over, in part a concession to popular emotional needs, the inner worship is a yogic means to transcend dualistic perception by the refining of the sense of sight, as described above. As such it comes under the category of 'meditation' and is one of a number of devices to focus the vacillating mind, and enter into the subtle strata of the object of focus until the trinity of seer, seen and seeing is transcended. The individual worshipper, through the medium of an imagined 'other' – the image – is led to experience his own unbounded, divine nature.

It is this process in reverse that the artist employs in receiving the archetypal form he is to depict. The first two Sutras of Chapter 4 of the *Vastu Sutra Upanishad* tell us: '*From the realization comes the symbol. From the form of the symbol arise the limbs of the image.*' The commentary expands these two cryptic sentences:

Formerly there was Absolute Consciousness only, the One and the Truth. When this Absolute is experienced in meditation it is as the pure light within

Shiva's trident (*trishula*) symbolizing the three-in-one at the heart of creation.

the space of the heart. . . . When the mind is thus fully expanded, that is the Absolute without qualities. As a conception arises, it is the Absolute with qualities taking form. From this form the mind materializes.

In other words, the visualization of the image within the mind of the artist emerges in three stages. First, the mind is expanded through meditation to utter silence, a transcendental state of pure Consciousness, beyond any activity of thought or feeling. From the silence of this innermost depth of subjectivity, the mind takes shape as an archetypal symbol, abstract still, but manifesting into form. From here the third stage, the manifest image, is born, and it is this which is projected into the medium to be worked. This spontaneous emergence of form renders the artist a passive and receptive channel of a divine archetype which emerges, unfolding like a flower, from an abstract seed to a fully opened bloom.

The worshipper has an array of visual devices to serve his inner worship. Figurative three-dimensional images express the concrete form of divine beings; more abstract geometrical diagrams in two dimensions – some circular (*mandala*; *chakra*) others linear (*yantra*) – depict the constituent forces that compose the images, being, in effect, their abstract, or subtle, bodies. All of these forms are perfectly congruous, being but different gradations of the same Reality. Each can be used as a focus from which the mind ascends in contemplation; and as such they are springboards to the experience of that boundless Unified Field which we in truth are, as is the whole world when viewed aright. In the words of a celebrated Vedantic text, the *Yoga Vasishtha Ramayana*: 'Man should not take the name of Vishnu without himself becoming Vishnu, nor worship Vishnu without becoming Vishnu, nor remember Vishnu without becoming Vishnu.'

The texts lay down all the details which are conducive to this realization: the correct height of the devotee's seat, the material of which it should be made, the direction it should face, the time and place of worship, and so on. So vast is the Hindu material on this that there is considerable variety in these rules; nevertheless if one path is faithfully followed it is believed to be efficacious for the particular type of worship in question.

The inner worship has itself two stages. After the requisite purification, the devotee first practises meditation in which he reconstructs the image internally on the level of consciousness. In this he mimics the contemplation practised by the artist, opening his silent mind to allow an archetypal form to emerge from its depths. Only when this has been successfully accomplished is the mental form of the deity projected into the image, in which objective form it can now be worshipped. A devotional text called 'The Swelling Stream of Bliss of the Believer in Shakti' (*Shaktanandataragini*) tells us:

> Those who seek the *devata* without, forsaking the *devata* within, are like a man who wanders around looking for glass after throwing away the precious *kaustabha* jewel that he held in his hand. After seeing the chosen divinity in one's heart, one should establish Her in the image, picture, vessel or *yantra* and then worship her.

An image is thus nothing in itself unless vivified by consciousness. Its worship is actually a means by which we are tricked into experiencing the overlooked reality of our everyday perception as a process in which the divine unity endlessly contemplates itself in its voluntarily assumed disguise of duality.

The second, final stage of image worship moves to an internalization of the whole process, when the outer form of the *deva* as image is replaced by the inner form of a being vibrant in consciousness alone. This last step is explained by Vishnu himself in the *Bhagavata Purana*:

> A yogi will call to mind within the circle of fire in the lotus of his heart this form of mine, beneficial in meditation – namely a form full-limbed, calm, of beautiful features, with four long and beautiful arms; graceful neck and a fair forehead; with divine and gracious smile; adorned with brilliant ear ornaments in his two well-shaped ears; dressed in yellow or deep blue; ... bearing in his four hands a conch shell, a discus, a club and a lotus; with a garland of flowers on his breast; with lotus feet shining with the lustre of bejewelled anklets ... ornamented with shining crown, bracelets, waist-chain and armlets; beauteous in all limbs, pleasant; his countenance sweet with grace, with tender gaze and form fair to look upon.

Vishnu goes on to say that the mediator should 'bathe his mind completely in the waters of love for Me' and then hold this inner image until he can comfortably fix his attention on one part of it. From here he should then transfer his inner gaze to the deity's face. From uninterrupted contemplation of the divine face, the mind can expand to embrace the infinite. 'Then it will not be necessary to meditate on anything', for the worshipper will see the essence of the deity as his own, essential, Self, as 'one light mingled with another'.

Hanuman, the flying monkey-god, is the epitome of devotion: loyal, courageous and resourceful. In the *Ramayana*, he serves as the general of Rama, who, as king of Ayodhya, is the embodiment of righteousness. In his campaign to rescue Sita, his master's wife, from the clutches of Ravana, the ten-headed demon who has abducted her, Hanuman symbolizes the rescue of the soul from the clutches of egoism.
(Folk shrine of Hanuman, Ujjain)

Everything is born from the infinitely creative Void, the cosmic no-thing-ness; by the Void everything is maintained, and into the Void it eventually returns. As the Divine Mother of all things, the Void is here represented as the supreme Goddess (*above left*) with a space left empty for her image. But the Void is also our own unbounded nature, the ground of our being, beyond the threshold of our normal awareness, beyond all thought and feeling, located

deep in the cave of the heart. Meditation, traditionally practised in grottoes or rock-cut sanctuaries (*above right*), is the path to discover within ourselves this eternal reality, of which all life is but the temporary and non-binding expression like the ocean's waves. (*Above left:* The supreme Goddess as the plenum-Void, Andhra Pradesh, 19th century; *above right:* The Vedic gods Surya and Indra flank the entrance to a cell at Bhaja, mid-2nd century BC)

As the light of life, fire is the brilliance of intelligence, the ardour of strength and the glow of health. It is also the energy of passion, of anger and lust. Indeed, the very universe is the result of the spark of divine desire, the One wishing to be many. In Vedic worship fire is personified as the god Agni and known as 'the All-Possessor', 'the Purifier', 'the Resplendent', and

Vedic priests cast offerings of clarified butter, oil, and grain into the ritual fire to propitiate the unseen celestial intelligences that govern life. In Hinduism, light is offered to the image of deities, as a symbol of our own individual consciousness, and the enlightenment which is its fulfilment. Householders are married with the sacred fire as a witness; they should always keep a fire burning in the home, and honour the ancestors with fire. The daily routine of the orthodox begins with worshipping the sun as the source of life, while yogic ascetics fire-walk to prove their mastery over the elements. Fire not only creates and sustains life, it eventually consumes it: cremation is the final rite of sacrifice. As the *Brihadaranyaka Upanishad* (c. 800 BC) says, 'Into fire the gods offer the body of man. From this oblation a new being arises, who has the brilliance of light.'

(*Left:* A priest at ritual worship (*puja*) of the Goddess Durga part of which is the offering of light; *below left:* A woman at her hearth; *below:* Spring fire-walking ceremony at Phalen, to ensure good crops)

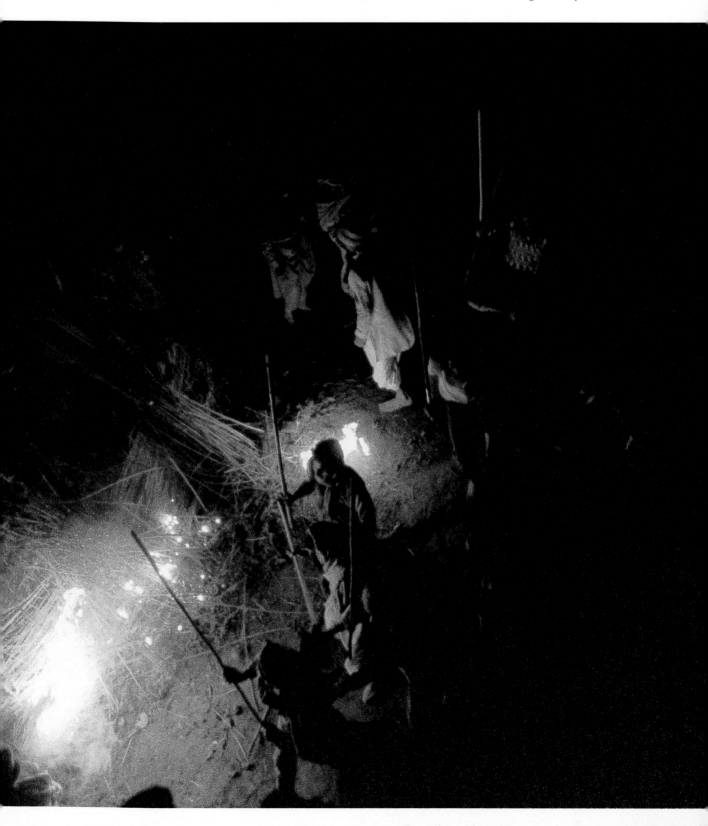

Some of the most profound aspects of Hindu thought are linked with Shiva, 'the Auspicious One'. He is the god personifying pure transcendence; he is the boundless, silent substratum of all manifestation, standing alone, prior to all time, space and causation. 'Thou art not lit by the light of the sun, nor by the light of the moon, nor by stars, nor by lightning, and much less still by fire' (*Shvetashvatara Upanishad*).

In this primal, abstract state Shiva is represented as the *lingam* ('emblem'), the phallic-shaped stone which stands for the immovable majesty of the Absolute, and expresses its eternal, indestructible power. But Shiva cannot create alone: it is only in union with the *yoni* ('womb' or 'vagina'), symbol of the feminine principle, which holds the *lingam* in its grasp, that creation can take place.

(*Below:* Shiva's bull Nandi looks down over *yoni-lingams* lapped by the sacred waters of the Ganges at Varanasi; *right:* Eka-mukha-lingam, a *lingam* with a face representing the great god Shiva, 5th century AD)

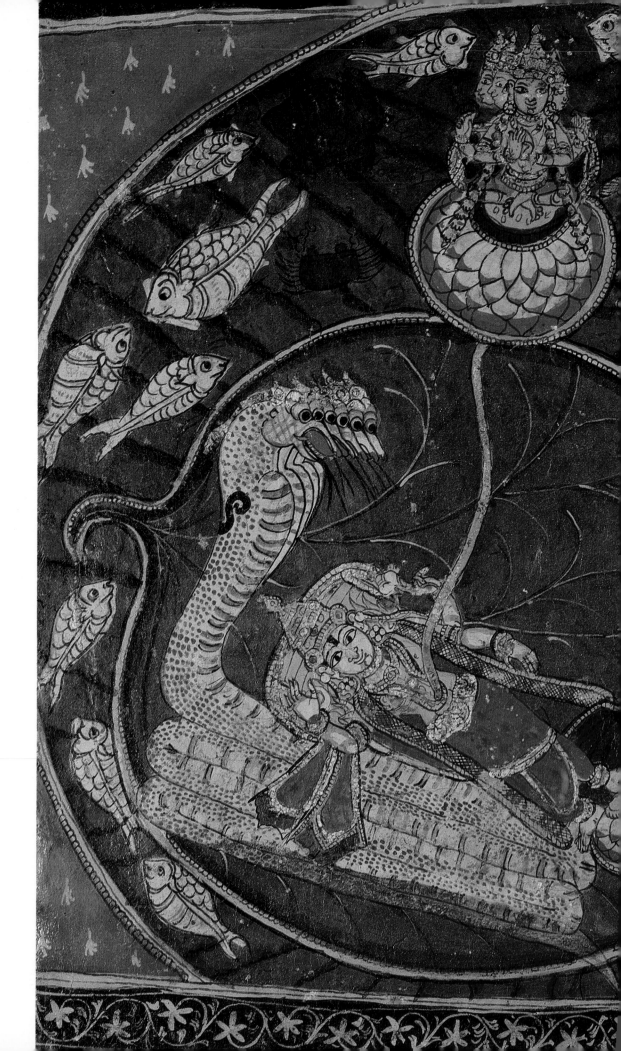

The Hindu vision of time as a conception to measure eternity is enormously expansive. Time proceeds through innumerable cycles of manifestation and disintegration: the present age of degeneracy, Kali Yuga, lasting 432,000 human years, is relatively short. Among the many creation myths one is particularly popular, especially in South India. In between cycles of manifestation when the universe dissolves, Vishnu 'the All-Pervading' exists in his form as Narayana, 'lying on the causal waters'. He reclines asleep on the serpent Ananta-shesha, 'the Infinite Remainder', a symbolic embodiment of all the residual tendencies of action and re-action created by the last cycle. These will, in time, determine the form of the next cycle, as the seed determines the form of the tree. As Vishnu sleeps, he dreams, and in his dream a lotus emerges from his navel, unfolding to reveal Brahma, god of creation, sitting in its pericarp. Brahma has four heads and four arms, representing the four directions and the sacred scriptures, the four *Vedas*. From these the universe is ordered in space and time, and a new cycle of manifestation is set to begin once more.

(*Left:* Vishnu-Narayana, South India, 18th century AD)

The Hindu artist has a marvellous ability to depict the essential quality of his subject, particularly when he is working in stone. For all the abstract levels of meaning that can be extracted from many of these works, scenes of everyday living are often rendered with a naturalistic empathy that is breathtaking. Typically, the graceful flowing contours of human figures display the languid suppleness of plant forms, an affinity that is not only pleasing aesthetically but emphasizes the richness of a life well lived, nurtured by an awareness that recognizes and celebrates the unity of all life. This unitive vision is here shown to inform both of the complementary and mutually interdependent poles between which Hindu social life is structured: the householder, whose activity stabilizes and continues the material aspect of life, and the recluse who silently works to provide spiritual leaven to the society he has renounced. Whether in the tenderness of the human and the sensual, or in the austerity of that endeavour which seeks to transcend the limited realms of sensory pleasure and mundane possibilities, life is naturally full.

(*Above left:* Motherhood, Khajuraho, 12th century AD; *above right:* Loving couple (*maithuna*), Khajuraho, 10th century AD; *right:* Ascetic worshipping the sun, Mahabalipuram, 7th century AD)

The *devas* are luminous energies which inhabit the subtle and astral levels that both inform and transcend the gross physical levels of reality in which our awareness is normally confined. But they are not only celestial beings external to us: they operate in and through us, and manifest as our own possibilities of being and behaving. As such they are the patient

archetypes of our own potential, hidden deep within the subtle levels of daily life. Indeed, we are all already gods and goddesses of a sort, for we create, maintain and destroy: to beings further down the evolutionary ladder, at least, we no doubt appear godlike. The purifying disciplines of self-transcendence — worship, service, meditation, the arts — are the channels through which human activity enters the realm of the divinities, and becomes an expression of their blessing.

Durga, 'the one beyond reach', was created by the fiery thought-forms of the other gods to restore righteousness on earth. With her royal mount the lion, the form of the great Goddess here (*above*) personifies the terrible power of good, her many hands and arms symbolizing her many aspects and attributes. The enemy of good is egoism in all its forms, here (*left*) represented by Ravana, the ten-headed demon.

(*Above:* A Durga shrine incorporating images of straw and clay made for the annual Durga Puja festival, Varanasi; *left:* An actor impersonates Ravana in the Ram Lila play based on the *Ramayana*, Varanasi)

Once the sculptor has chosen the deity to be portrayed, he recites the verses from the ancient scriptures – *Vedas*, *Puranas* and *Shastras* – describing that deity. Then he meditates, waiting in stillness for an image to appear in his mind, which, when it arrives, is drawn rapidly, lest the movement of thought interfere with it. Then a piece of stone that has the right 'tone' is chosen, ritually prepared to be a fit receptacle for the deity, and the light, deft touch of hammer and chisel on hard stone rings out like music. The last feature to be sculpted is the eyes. Then life-energy is breathed into the stone in a special rite known as *prana pratishtha*, by which the image is imbued with consciousness and becomes a vital channel for the descent of the divine energies and the dissemination of their blessings into the community.

Reciprocally, the image acts as a means of self-transcendence for the worshipper. Symbols of the five senses – chanting, food, light, water and flowers – are offered to the deity in a rite which, by cultivating feelings of loving surrender, allows the devotee to ascend to that inner reality which lies beyond the senses.

(*Right:* Shiva, Varanasi; *far right:* A woman tends a wayside Hanuman shrine at Varanasi)

To the Hindu artist, tradition, when fully internalized and absorbed, is not a straitjacket, but a means to freedom, bestowing the benefits of a common language of form and the liberation of great emotional power. The inherited body of images, postures and attributes serves to articulate that shared imaginative terrain which links society to the Divine, an area that is collectively analogous to the intermediate world of fantasy which the individual child establishes between itself as an isolated body-ego and its increasingly distant mother. Here the baby Krishna (*right*), representing the blissful and irrepressible spontaneity of life, dances beside an image of Parvati, 'the Lady of the Mountain', the great Goddess in her benign or peaceful form (*far right*). As Shiva's consort, Parvati is the idealized feminine: nurturing and gentle, portrayed with the full breasts, wasp-like waist and wide hips of a graceful fertility icon. Symbolizing the material substance of life, she holds in her right hand a lotus bud that alludes to the fecundity of Nature, while between the thumb and forefinger of her left hand, the entire universe hangs suspended. Both figures wear the jewelry and headdresses of royalty, as befits their status, and both rest on a lotus, symbol of purity and creative energy.
(Bronzes made by the lost-wax method, typical of the highly accomplished Chola school of Tanjore, South India, which flourished between the late 10th and 13th centuries AD)

The mediator between the deities and humanity is the hereditary priestly caste known as the *brahmins*, who traditionally enjoy supreme status (though not necessarily temporal power or wealth) in Hindu society. Paradoxically, some shrines of great folk antiquity are looked after by priests from other castes, even the lowest. Within the complex hierarchy of temple organization, different groups of *brahmins* have different functions: some prepare food for offerings, some clean and dress the images, some present certain offerings, others chant the scriptures in Sanskrit, the priestly language. *Brahmins* are also the custodians of all traditional learning: astrology, mathematics, the arts, medicine and so on. As India follows the West in moving away from traditional religious belief into the world of science and materialism, orthodox *brahmins* are having radically to reassess their role in modern secular life.

Here a priest (*below*), with the front of his head shaven in the South Indian manner, distributes among worshippers the blessings (*prasad*) of light and food that have been offered to the deity, while temple priests and musicians (*right*) rest before hymning a processional image of Shiva and Parvati sitting on the sacred bull Nandi.

Many of the holiest Hindu shrines have as their main image an unworked stone or piece of wood, testifying to the primordial power of the Supreme, which, independent of any human artifice, is always offering epiphanies to those with the child-like openness to see them. In Puri, on the Bay of Bengal, the mighty temple dedicated to Krishna as Jagannatha ('Lord of the Universe') enshrines three such *swyambhu* ('self-created') images: of Krishna, his brother Bala Rama and his sister Subadhra. Among the holiest in India, they are believed to have been carved by none other than Vishvakarman, the divine architect and sculptor, disguised as an old man, from a log, washed up by the sea, whose whereabouts was revealed to the patron, King Indradyumna, in a dream.

(*Above:* Doll-like models of the trio stand against a wall at Puri painted with Vaishnava subjects – Vishnu with his mace symbolizing the power of knowledge, pots of basil which is sacred to the god, and the *amrita kalash*, the 'pot containing the elixir of immortality'; *right:* An ancient fertility deity, Calcutta)

The Hindu pantheon is an attempt to define and classify the basic energies that conduct the universe. Since all the energies at the origin of all the forms of manifestation are but aspects of the One divine creative power, there is no form of existence which is not ultimately divine in its nature. Thus Hindu mythology acknowledges all gods, all forms, all possibilities, reaching far beyond the limitations of rationality with an unequalled imaginative boldness. To depict these energies as deities, demigods and demons, a living body of dream-like images has evolved over five thousand years, incorporating

the various cultural strands of a country as large and as diverse as Europe. The cosmic escapades of the deities comprise archetypal myths and legends that have been the medium of popular education since time immemorial, and are considered to have the same exemplary value that the West ascribes to history. This tradition provides Hindu culture with a striking visual continuity between the modern world of film-posters and television and the ancient world of temple and shrine. (Inexpensive contemporary popular prints of gods and goddesses, mass-produced in Bombay)

Devotees at the feet of Surya, the Sun-God, who was one of the three chief deities in Vedic times, though less worshipped today. As the celestial form of fire, Surya is the source of all energy and light on earth; as the origin of time he is the father of Yama ('the Binder'), Lord of Death, who keeps mankind in check. Surya represents the limit of our life, the point where the manifest and unmanifest worlds meet. He rides enthroned on a lotus in a one-wheeled chariot which is guided by his charioteer Aruna ('the Dawn'), who shields the world from the sun's fury. It is pulled across the sky each day by seven golden horses, symbolizing the seven sages who govern the heavenly constellations. Both church and state bow down before the omnipotent source of all life, to whom, in the words of the *Brihadaranyaka Upanishad*, 'the priests and the warriors are but food, and death is but a sauce'. At Surya's left foot kneels the shaven-headed priest; at his right the king, his sword laid down in submission. This royal figure may well be Narasingha, a great warrior who built the Sun Temple at Konarak (from where this image comes) to commemorate his victory over the Muslims. Beside the devotees stand Surya's two bearded attendants, Dandi and the pot-bellied Pingala, themselves flanked by armed guards. The faces of all the figures radiate *ananda*, that sweet blissfulness believed by the Hindus to be the nature of life itself. (Detail of the south face of the Sun Temple at Konarak, Orissa, mid-13th century AD)

The enduring matrix of the organic
world is the vast background
against which humanity is always
set in Hindu thought and art. Our
strength comes from cooperating
with Nature, not subduing her, for
violence done to animals and
plants is violence done to
ourselves: there is no separation in
the seamless web of life. But this
matrix is also the theatre of the
mind turned inside-out, for Nature,
the goddess Prakriti ('evolving
action'), includes everything that
is not spirit alone, stretching from
life in its densest expressions as
relatively inanimate matter through
vegetal and animal forms to
mankind and the realms of spirits,
angels and the gods. Within this
range of life exists a huge and
extraordinary retinue of fellow
creatures, many fantastic and
otherworldly from the human point
of view, but worthy to be known as
living intimately alongside us,
members of our imaginative
heritage congregating along our
path to the Supreme. Some of
these beings guard the threshold
of temple, shrine and our own
unconscious depths; others are
oneiric hybrids, spanning the
daylight boundaries of element and
species. They can be helpers, and
should be acknowledged without
fear, for they are but manifestations
of our own essential nature, and
accepting them will help us to love
and know ourselves.

(*Above left:* A ram, on the
Brahmeshvara Temple,
Bhubaneshvar, 11th century AD,
and a temple-guarding *yali* on the
Vaikuntha Perumal Temple,
Kanchipuram, 8th century AD; *below
left:* a *makara*, mythological sea-
dragon and guardian of the depths,
Halebid, 12th century AD; *above
right:* Nandikeshvara, vehicle of
Shiva in human form with a bull's
head, one of the mythical teachers
of music and dancing, on the
Adinatha Jaina Temple, Khajuraho,
10th century AD; *below right:* Naga
serpent king, custodian of esoteric
knowledge, Phimeanakas, Angkor
Wat, Cambodia, 12th century AD)

The *Mahabharata* is one of the great epics that have inspired Hindus for countless generations. It tells the story of a historical war between two families, the Pandavas and the Kauravas, but in such a way that history itself is seen as a symbol of the inner laws that rule humanity. Thus the war is also the expression of the eternal battle between good and evil, or the gods and the demons, and simultaneously an account of the corresponding inner struggle within the lives of every man and woman.

One of the five Pandava brothers, who symbolize the forces of good, is Bhima, 'the Tremendous'. Epitomizing strength and fortitude, he is commander of the Pandava army in the *Bhagavad Gita* ('the Song of God'), which is the eighteenth chapter of the *Mahabharata*, and one of the most popular Hindu scriptures. Bhima is a great folk hero, especially in North India, and his exploits are considered part of the response of Nature herself to the imbalance created by the preponderance of evil at the time of the Mahabharata war.

(Folk images of Bhima made out of mud on the banks of the Ganges at Varanasi, for the autumn festival of Bhima Puja)

In Vedic thought, sound and form are inseparable. The universe is seen as a complex and dynamic web of interdependent relationships, a continuous dance of vibrating energy-forms, each of which, from the harmony of the spheres to the vibrations of molecules and atoms, has its own movement, rhythm and constituent sounds. Man is not only formed of sound vibrations, but lives and moves in them; they surround him as a fish is surrounded by water. Knowledge of these sounds and their effects is the science of *mantra*, through which the rhythms of life can be utilized to best advantage, and both the subtle and gross levels of matter be affected. The Sanskrit language is believed to be the nearest the human tongue can approximate to 'the language of natural name', those root-

syllables which are the constituent sounds of the universe, and the Sanskrit scriptures constitute an oral tradition of wisdom that has been passed down by word of mouth from generation to generation.

Chanting the many names of God has a purifying effect on both the nervous system and the atmosphere, and in Vedic ritual the correct use of *mantras* will attract the deities whose sound-bodies they are. Used correctly, sound can unfurl the finest petals of feeling and transport the mind to that silence which is the mother of all sounds.

(*Below left:* A priest chants the scriptures; *below right:* Chanters sit wrapped in prayer-shawls inscribed with praises of Ram, one of the most popular names of the Supreme)

Themes

'The waves constituting the
universe spontaneously arise and
disappear in you, who are yourself
the unbounded ocean of
Consciousness. You suffer no loss
or gain' (*Ashtavakra Gita*).
(Riverside shrine beside the Ganges,
containing Nandi, *yoni-lingam* and
deity)

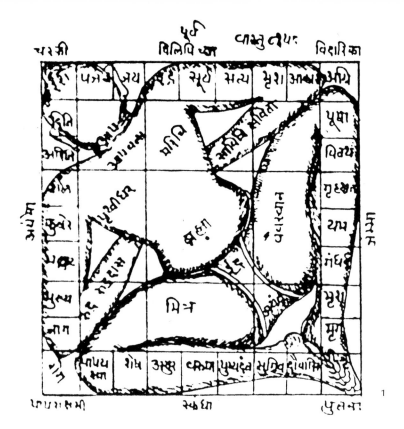

Hinduism arose from the ashes of the Vedic civilization, whose recondite depths remain tantalizingly unfathomed by Western scholarship. 'Truth is one, though the sages call it by many names' says the *Rig Veda*, one of the four *Vedas*, scriptures accepted by orthodox Hindus, whose religion still contains many vestiges of Vedic teaching.

One of the Vedic creation myths personalizes the supreme Consciousness as Purusha, the Cosmic Man, who by his self-sacrifice gives birth to the universe. Since the temple is the universe in miniature, its groundplan is drawn as a grid formed by the body of Purusha [1]. His navel is its unmoving centre, the various parts of his body the gods that structure manifestation. Similar groundplans existed for domestic buildings.

The Vedic seers hymned the causal energies of the world as various deities. Three are pre-eminent. Agni [2] mediates between men and gods, and presides over sacraments. He is intelligence, light and fire and carries fans to kindle the flames of the

sacrificial offerings. His vehicle is the ram. Indra, king of the gods [3], rules the sky. He is associated with rain and fertility; electrical energy is his thunderbolt. He governs sacrifice; his vehicle is the bull. Surya [4] is the sun, the centre, origin of warmth and life, the point where the unmanifest manifests.

The heart of the Vedic civilization was not the images that were to become so important in Hinduism, but fire rituals (yagyas), by which the harmony between the celestial and terrestrial realms was preserved. In these the fire-pit [5] became the universe in miniature, and the subtle intelligences that govern life were invoked by chanting and propitiated by offering substances such as grain, milk and clarified butter.

1 *Purushamandala*, from an ancient manual of temple architecture.
2 Agni. South India, 17th century.
3 Indra. South India, 17th century.
4 Surya. Hoyshala style, 13th century.
5 Fire-pit for Vedic yagya. Maharashtra, modern.

The Vedic Vision

3

4

5

The most enigmatic of the major deities is Shiva, 'the Auspicious', an extraordinarily rich character, in whom are met all the contradictory aspects of human nature. He is the joyful Lord of the universal Dance and fiery destroyer of demons; archetypal celibate yogi and drunken seducer of the sages' wives; haunter of funeral grounds and embodiment of irrepressible vitality.

Shiva's most comprehensive form is as Nataraja, 'Lord of the Dance' [6]. Encircled by endless fire symbolizing creation and transformation, he is a figure of Dionysian abandon, breaking all boundaries with his 'dance of bliss'. His hair, in which float all the planets, streams out wildly; his lower right hand signifies 'fear not', while his upper right holds the *damaru*, the hour-glass shaped drum whose beating is the pulse of time. In his upper left hand he holds fire, symbol of his transforming energy, while his fourth hand points nonchalantly down to his upraised foot, before which all must bow. Shiva tramples the demon of ignorance, the self-centred ego that must be transcended for realization to dawn.

As the essential interdependence of spirit and matter, Shiva is abstracted into the *yoni-lingam* [7]. His fierce

6

7

8

9

aspect, Bhairava, the terrible destroyer of demons [8], is also the right head of Mahadeva, 'the Great God' [9], whose central head is Shiva in his own nature and the left one Uma, his peaceful *shakti*. Shiva with his consort Parvati, as a loving couple, is a popular symbol of wholeness [10]. Here he holds the axe of discrimination, as he does in the boldest statement of the intrinsic unity of all life, the hermaphrodite Ardhanarishvara ('the Lord who is half-woman') [12], a single figure in which the complimentary qualities of male and female are beautifully combined, and their division transcended.

6 Shiva Nataraja. South-east India, 11th–12th century.
7 *Yoni-lingam*. Allahabad, modern.
8 Bhairava. Tribal, Rajasthan, 17th century.
9 Shiva Mahadeva. Elephanta Island, 8th century.
10 Shiva and Parvati. Tanjore, 12th century.
11 Shiva as Dakshinamurti, the archetypal spiritual teacher. South India, 10th century.
12 Ardhanarishvara. South India, 11th century.

10

11

12

Vishnu and Brahma

14

15

13

16

17

18

Vishnu ('the All-Pervading') is the preserver of life: he embodies the power of cohesion within the supreme Consciousness. As such he is associated with the refinement of feelings and with activity in the world. He is pre-eminently the deity of householders, with followers known as Vaishnavas.

A popular creation myth features Vishnu as Narayana [13] who reclines on the serpent Ananta ('Infinity') afloat on the causal waters. As Narayana dreams, a lotus arises from his navel, bearing Brahma ('the Immensity') [14], the personification of the creative principle inherent in Consciousness. Little worshipped today, Brahma has four heads – four being the number of the earth – which order the universe into the four cardinal directions, and four arms which refer to the four *Vedas* and the four aims of the householder's life: duty, success, refinement and liberation. His consort, Saraswati ('the Flowing One') [15], represents the organizing power of intelligence; she is the deity of speech, knowledge, learning and the arts. She plays the stringed *vina*, from whose notes arise the root-sounds of the Sanskrit language by which the whole universe is structured.

There are twenty-four forms of Vishnu, some associated with specific places or temples. He is dark blue, the colour of infinity, and is usually shown with four arms, extending the open palm of generosity, and holding the solar disc (symbolizing the life-giving sun) and the conch (origin of the five elements); in the fourth, he may be shown with either a mace (the power of time) or a lotus (creativity). Here [16] he is flanked by his two consorts: to his left, the bare-breasted goddess Bhu-devi ('the Earth'), to his right the goddess Shri-devi ('Good Fortune'). His vehicle is Garuda ('Wings of Speech') [17], the man-bird hybrid who is indomitable courage. Shri is also known as Lakshmi ('She of the hundred-thousands') [17,18], who herself has eight forms, in any one of which she is popularly worshipped as the deity of wealth.

13 Vishnu Narayana. Deogarh, 5th century.
14 Brahma. South India. 10th–11th century.
15 Saraswati. Madras, 19th century.
16 Vishnu with Shri-devi and Bhu-devi. South India, 19th century.
17 Vishnu, Lakshmi and Garuda. Shrirangam, early 20th century.
18 Lakshmi. Vijayanagar, 16th century.

71

The Great Goddess

The many forms of the Goddess range from archaic blood sacrificial deities to sophisticated symbols of the universal feminine, the life energy *shakti*. One school, Tantra, places great emphasis on the worship of the feminine principle in all its manifestations, including women in ritualized sexual yoga. Goddess images are some of the most powerful in Hindu iconography.

In a temple dedicated to Mother Divine, a tantric devotee is shown worshipping the Goddess by drinking from her *yoni* [19]. Another remarkable shrine to Mother Earth, who is Prithivi ('the Widely-Spread One'), emphasizes the instinctive nature of the deity by showing her with vegetation in place of a head [20], while an ancient terracotta plaque of a female fertility deity [21] shows exquisite detail in her moulded finery, which no doubt mimics the contemporary dress of the nobility. Such images are among many common to both Buddhism and Hinduism, being drawn from a vast pan-Indian reservoir of imaginative life that transcends sectarian boundaries.

Mother Divine is not only the benign nurturer of life; she can be wildly unpredictable, bringing disease, flood, famine and death. Even today, smallpox is known in Indian villages as 'the kiss of the Goddess'. This awesome power is represented above all by Kali ('the Black One') [22]. Her many arms show her many aspects; particularly noticeable are her hands with ritual dagger (lower right) and bowl made from a human skull (lower left) which catches sacrificial blood. Kali's general association with death – as emphasized by the skull in her headdress – is shared with her consort Shiva. Symbolically, she is time and all that tears asunder our attempts to resist change, the irresistible force of evolution. As the oldest stratum of Indian religion, Goddess worship often incorporates primeval fertility cults and exhibits the raw energy of animistic spirit worship [23]. At the other end of the *shakti* spectrum stands the graceful Parvati [24], as pure feminine energy, without which the masculine deity is powerless to create.

The feminine quality of solidarity, as exemplified in family and group, is shown by the Seven Mothers [25], earth goddesses who are the terrestrial counterpart of the nine planets, revered as sky deities.

19 Worship of the *yoni*. Madurai, 17th century.
20 The Goddess as the genetrix of all things. Hyderabad, 11th century.
21 *Yakshi* or Mother Goddess. Bengal, c. 200 BC.
22 Kali. South India, 12th century.
23 The terrible Karaikkalammai. South India, 12th century.
24 Parvati. Chola, 10th century.
25 The Seven Mothers. Perhaps Madhya Pradesh, 9th–10th century.

19

20

21

22　　　　　　　　　　　　　　　　　　　　　23　　24

25

26

28

29

27

30

The Major Incarnations of Vishnu

As Vishnu explains to Arjuna, the hero of the *Bhagavad Gita*: 'Whenever Truth decays and untruth flourishes, O noble one, then I create myself. To protect the righteous and destroy the wicked, to establish Truth firmly, I take birth age after age.' There are ten major such incarnations or *avatars* ('descents'), a phenomenon which is only a specific instance of the gods' general willingness, often reiterated in the Hindu scriptures, to make themselves accessible to humanity. The *avatars* trace the evolution of life on the planet.

In the Golden Age Vishnu incarnates four times. As Matsya the Fish [26] he saves Manu, the first Lawgiver, from the primal deluge; as Kurma the Tortoise [27] he helps in the churning of the primal waters which created *amrita*, Lakshmi goddess of Fortune, and the celestial nymphs; and as Varaha the Boar [28] he rescues the earth from the depths of the primordial ocean, divides it into seven continents, and endows it with life. The fourth incarnation, Narasingha, the 'Man-Lion' [29], was created to defeat a demon who beat and tortured his son, an ardent worshipper of Vishnu, in an attempt to stop his devotion. Due to a boon he had won from Brahma years before, the demon could not be killed by god, man or beast, by day or by night, neither inside nor outside his palace. So Vishnu becomes a hybrid creature, attacks the demon at twilight, on the threshold of his palace, and is thus able to disembowel him.

In the Silver Age, Vishnu becomes Vamana the Dwarf [30], who retrieves the universe from the clutches of the demon Bali. Vamana appears before

Bali and asks for as much land as he can cover in three strides. Derisively, the demon agrees; then the dwarf, expanding his size, covers the earth with his first step, the heavens with his second, and pushes Bali down to the nether regions with his third. The sixth incarnation is as Parashu Rama ('Rama with the Axe') [31] who defeats the *kshatriya* warrior caste and re-establishes priestly control over the monarchy. The seventh incarnation is Rama ('the Charming') [32], the embodiment of righteousness, whose rule over the kingdom of Ayodhya was an exemplary time of justice, peace and happiness.

In the Copper Age, Vishnu becomes Krishna (see pp. 76–7). In the present Iron Age – Kali Yuga or 'the Age of Darkness' – Vishnu incarnated as Buddha [33], whose teachings once illuminated much of Asia. The tenth and last incarnation, Kalki [34], is yet to come; riding a white horse and brandishing a flaming sword, he will destroy the world and establish a new Golden Age in its ashes.

26 Matsya. Pahari, 18th century.
27 Kurma. Bombay or Gujarat, 1801.
28 Varaha. North-east India, 9th–10th century.
29 Narasingha. Halebid, 12th century.
30 Vamana. Eastern India, 10th century.
31 Parashu Rama destroying the *kshatriyas*. Kangra school, late 19th century.
32 Rama seated with his virtuous wife Sita ('Nature') and his brother Lakshmana. Kangra school, late 19th century.
33 Buddha. Sarnath, 6th century.
34 Kalki. Madras, 19th century.

35

36

38

37

76

Krishna

Krishna, 'the Dark One', is the eighth and most important incarnation of Vishnu and the embodiment of love. He represents that unfettered spontaneity of life [35] which is above all manifest in love, the great unifier. Especially popular in North India, he is believed to have lived around Vrindavan, and the pastoral idyll of his youth represents a vision of the natural fullness of life. Supported by nature's bounty embodied in the cow, and sporting in the enchanted forest groves, Krishna characteristically upsets all predictable limits.

As a child [36] he naughtily steals milk and butter from the cowherds, or upsets their milk churns; as an adolescent [37] he defeats the snake-demon Kaliya, who has poisoned a village well, by dancing on his head. As a young man he is often portrayed as Venugopala, 'the cowherd with the flute' [38], pacifying all the animals of the forest with his sweet playing.

Krishna's captivating beauty drives the cowgirls mad with desire [39], and he mischievously breaks all the rules of social propriety with his amorous exploits. But he has a favourite, Radha ('Success'), and the story of their love is one of the world's great mystico-erotic poems. The whole tender and passionate range of human feelings is

symbolized by the *ras-lila* dance they
perform beneath the full moon [40],
while, on another level, their love is
a sublime metaphor for the soul's
unending longing for the true Beloved,
for God.

Krishna becomes the charioteer
of the righteous Pandavas in their
struggle against evil, depicted in the
Bhagavad Gita, where he teaches the
noble archer Arjuna meditation as the
way to transcend suffering and attain
the unitive vision. In the course of this
instruction, Krishna reveals himself in
his cosmic form [41] as the omni-
present Supreme, harmonizing all the
differences of life and 'blazing with the
splendour of a thousand suns'.

35 Krishna as a baby, sucking his toe
as an image of infinity. Tamil Nadu,
17th–18th century.
36 Bala Krishna, the child stealing the
butter. South India, 19th century.
37 Krishna Kaliyana. South India,
19th century.
38 Venugopala. South India, 17th
century.
39 'The Hour of Cow-Dust'. Kangra
school, 18th century.
40 The *ras-lila*. Jaipur school, *c*. 1800.
41 Krishna displaying his cosmic form.
Rajasthan, 18th century.

39

40   41

42

43

45

The Sons of Shiva

46

One day when Shiva was away, Parvati took a bath. Fearing she might be disturbed, she fashioned a child out of the soap suds and set him outside her chamber door as a guard. Shiva returned unexpectedly, and, learning that his wife was bathing, came to join her. The child-guard forbade him entrance despite his pleadings. Furious, Shiva burned off the head of the impudent child with a glance of his third eye. Emerging from her bath, Parvati was distraught. Just as Shiva vowed to replace the head with that of the first creature he saw, an elephant came lumbering into the courtyard; Shiva removed its head with a single blow of his trident, and set it on the child's body. Thus was born elephant-headed Ganesh ('Lord of Categories').

A plump, crafty and lovable trickster, Ganesh can remove obstacles if propitiated, and is the god of good beginnings. He helps any project, should be worshipped before the other deities, and guards the threshold of home and sanctuary.

Ganesh has several forms. As *swayambhu* ('Self-created') he appears in stones shaped in his likeness [42]. He carries his broken-off tusk, with which he writes down the epics, an elephant-goad to chasten his devotees, and the sweets he loves to eat, and he is accompanied by his vehicle, the tiny mouse [43]. He can be shown sitting [44], dancing [45] or standing [46], and is particularly popular in Western India.

Shiva's other son is Karttikeya ('Godson of the Pleiades') [47]; also known as Kumara ('the Adolescent'), Skanda ('the Jet of Semen'), Subrahmaniam ('Dear to the Brahmins') and Murugan ('the Boy') [48]. He rides a peacock who devours the poisoning serpent of time. Karttikeya is beautiful, but impulsive and warlike; he carries a spear and other weapons. Worshipped almost exclusively in South India, he is the god of war and chastity; women should not worship him.

42 *Swayambhu* Ganesh. Aurangabad, undated.
43 Ganesh. Agra, modern.
44 Tantric Ganesh. Blitar, Java, 13th century.
45 Dancing Ganesh. Halebid, 11th century.
46 Standing Ganesh. Madras, 10th century.
47 Six-headed Karttikeya with consorts. South India, 19th century.
48 Murugan. Madras, modern.

47

48

49

50

Attendants of the Gods

The approach to a god from the human level can be effected through his attendant or vehicle (*vahana*). These creatures embody some particular characteristic of their lord: thus Durga rides the fierce lion; Ganesh the crafty mouse; Saraswati the graceful swan. They also act as messenger or servant, conveying the supplication of the devotee to the heavenly court, and returning the divine grace to the worshipper.

Shiva's *vahana* is the bull Nandi ('the Joyous') [49], snow-white with red horns and golden trappings. He is instinctual power and adamantine strength. Shiva has many affinities with Dionysos; Nandi may originally have been part of a widespread ancient bull-cult, particularly preserved in the Minoan civilization of Crete.

Hanuman [50], the attendant of Lord Rama, is devotion and loyalty personified; his heart is always filled with Rama and Sita. It was Hanuman's courage (symbolized by his mace) which helped defeat king Ravana: the valiant monkey-god set fire to the demon's palace by leaping from roof to roof with a torch tied to his tail [53].

51

52

Vishnu and his consort Lakshmi are carried by Garuda ('Wings of Speech') [51,52] who represents the transporting power of sound, especially the hermetic utterances of the *Vedas*, of which his body is formed. Garuda can change his shape at will, but is depicted as half-bird, half-man, the colour of molten gold, with the head of an eagle, a red beak, feathered wings and a large belly with two arms like a man. He dwells in the 'land of gold' – the celestial realms of creation – and destroys the serpent of illusion. Once he stole the ambrosia of immortality from the gods to free his mother from the clutches of the serpent king. Indra, king of the gods, realized that even he could not defeat Garuda in battle, so he recovered the nectar by speaking sweetly to the mighty bird, and charmed it away from him.

49 Nandi. Mysore, 17th century.
50 Hanuman. Modern.
51 Garuda transporting Vishnu and Lakshmi. South India, 19th century.
52 Vishnu and Lakshmi riding on Garuda. Bundi school, 18th century.
53 Hanuman. Belur, 12th century.

53

Hinduism is at its heart a non-dual system, and thus does not share the Christian concept of absolute evil. Nevertheless, there is a formidable array of beings, forces of negativity, who serve as enemies of the light. These demons (asura = 'non-light') differ from the gods (sura) in degree rather than kind; indeed they can win boons from the gods by penance, and if they repent, may end up as great devotees, or benefactors of mankind.

Once Vishnu promised the defeated gods the elixir of immortality (amrita) if they would temporarily cooperate with the demons and churn the Ocean of Milk [54], using Mount Mandara as a churning stick and the serpent Vasuki as the churning rope. Vishnu himself, as a tortoise, acted as the pivot. From the churning arose the elixir which the gods drank gleefully.

Representative of the vast array of anti-gods – giants, genies, witches, serpents, raw flesh eaters, night prowlers and scaly agents of time – is the demoness Vatapi [55], who ill-treated the sages and was defeated by Agastya, the holy man who brought Vedic rites to South India.

A famous victory for good was the defeat of the genie king Mahisha, who took the form of a buffalo, symbol of death, and was decapitated by Durga [56]. Like many demons, the belligerent but stylish Ravana – epitomizing egoism and greed – can change his form at will, as shown by his ten heads and twenty arms [57]. At the climax of the Ramayana, he almost defeated Rama in single combat, but eventually Rama's magic weapon prevailed.

Everyone is at some time affected by Rahu ('the Seizer') [58] who tries to swallow the sun and moon at eclipses because they prevented him drinking the amrita when the ocean was churned. As the ascending node of the moon, Rahu causes many problems in the astrological horoscope, vitally important for the Hindu.

54 Churning the Ocean of Milk. Maharashtra, 18th century.
55 Vatapi. Mahakuteshwar, 6th century.
56 Durga slaying the buffalo-demon. Mahabalipuram, 8th century.
57 Ravana. South India, 19th century.
58 Rahu. Konarak, 13th century.
59 Hanuman attacks the gigantic demon Mainak. Varanasi, modern.

Enemies of the Gods

56

57

59

8

Fabulous Creatures

63

The stories that have enthralled Hindus since time immemorial feature not only the great gods and goddesses, but a vast array of demigods (*devatas*), spirits and fabulous creatures drawn from centuries of rich imaginative experience.

The *gandharvas* ('fragrances') [60] are the celestial harmonies, angelic beings whose vibrations soothe and nourish the earth plane. Amorous intelligences, the *gandharvas* like scented oils and incense, and they gave the gift of music to mankind. Their preferred instrument is the *vina*, whose sweet modes culture the refined emotions of love and devotion. The *charanas* ('wanderers') [61] are the panegyrists of the heavens. Their speciality is to recount the ancient tales, sing the praises of heroes and teach the arts of dance, at which they excel.

On the earth plane, the *ganas* ('categories') [62] are groups of elvish beings who protect mankind, and particularly the temple, against negative forces. They are part of Shiva's retinue and are under the command of Ganesh ('Lord of the *ganas*'). Serpent kings and queens (*nagas*) are half-snake, half-human [63]. They are beautiful, richly adorned and dangerous, and they defend their sumptuous underworld cities fiercely against both gods and men. They are the guardians of the scriptures and esoteric knowledge, and often live under water.

Many temple guardians are fabulous hybrids (*yalis*), often the heraldic emblem of the temple builder [64,65]. They combine various powerful creatures – dragons, elephants, lions, horses – and are usually shown with the pop-eyes of a god expecting blood sacrifice, destroying enemies.

60 *Gandharvas*. Badami, 6th century.
61 *Charana*. Ellora, 8th century.
62 *Gana* and lion mount. Kanchipuram, 8th century.
63 *Naga*. Konarak, 13th century.
64 *Yali* and elephants. Konarak, 13th century.
65 Heraldic lion. Mahabalipuram, 7th century.

64   65

66

67

69

68

70

If each object is nothing but the supreme intelligence temporarily localized in a form, then all life is sacred, and nature is constantly providing us with epiphanies. All the forces which structure life – the elements, the planets, the directions of space – are considered holy by Hindus, as are a large range of natural phenomena – plants, trees, mountains, rivers, berries, gemstones, metals. Their power can be utilized, for each object, being a particular grouping of constituent forces, has a specific effect on the vibrations of the human nervous system.

Many trees are considered sacred, being symbolic descendants of the *veda druma*, the archetypal Tree of Life and Knowledge [66]. This universal symbol refers esoterically to the human nervous system which holds the key to the secret of life. Here the five-headed snake sitting on the lotus symbolizes the life energy (*kundalini*), and its expression through the five senses. The lotus refers to the *chakras*, the nodes of energy in the subtle body, and, as a feminine symbol of creativity, is also the throne of the deities [67].

Trees such as the banyan [68] are sacred to Shiva; sacred to Vishnu are the *shalagramas* [69], black stones found on the bed of the Narmada River, that

contain ammonite fossils over two hundred million years old. The recondite form of the *shalagrama* evokes the idea of cosmic beginnings and the mysterious, silent power of the seed, while the coco-de-mer [70], a symbol of the Goddess as Mother Divine, simulates her earthly emblem, the vulva.

Life is naturally full, and redolent with that bliss (*ananda*) which gives to so much Hindu art its serene and sunny happiness. Blissful beings [72], especially loving couples [73] are common embellishments of caves, sanctuaries and temples. They radiate a harmonious balance with an effortless grace, flowering as virtual extensions of the natural world around them.

66 *Veda druma*, the Tree of Life and Knowledge. Vijayanagar, 15th century.
67 Detail of manuscript on *chakras*. Rajasthan, 18th century.
68 Banyan tree with shrine. Goa.
69 *Shalagrama*. Varanasi, modern.
70 Coco-de-mer. South India, 19th century.
71 Early morning ritual ablutions in the Ganges. Varanasi.
72 Blissful nymph. Konarak, 13th century.
73 Loving couple. Badami, 6th century.

72

73

The Folk Shrine

Sophisticated temples are characteristically urban in their emphasis, serving regional rather than local needs, and prey to the changes wrought by politics and time. But folk shrines continue as they always have done: simple, serene and intensely human. Representing two enduring and vital aspects of Indian society – its predominantly rural slant and its cultural and ethnic diversity – they cater to the needs of the village or small group, preserving an ancient animistic tradition that complements the high temple culture. Folk shrines are charged with the deepest hopes, fears and beliefs of millions. They are usually patronized by lower castes, and their officiating priests are often women or non-*brahmins*.

Village shrines are often linked to the primeval tree cult; stones stand for Mother Earth [74]. Snake-stones are worshipped by women wanting children [75]; infertility is believed to be the result of killing a snake in a previous life. Tree spirits (*yakshis*) [76] abound in both Hindu and Buddhist art, as fertility icons and protagonists in legends and myths.

74

75

76

77

In Tamil Nadu, the cult of Aiyannar, a protective god who patrols the village on horseback at night [77], is very widespread. Stone or terracotta horses are set up at the outskirts of the village, sometimes with the god and his attendants, sometimes riderless, and offerings, including blood sacrifice and alcohol, are made. The spirits influence all aspects of daily life; here a priest makes offerings at a shrine especially for rickshaw drivers, each of whom has donated a bell to the spirits [78].

The happy intermingling of the sophisticated and simple levels of Hinduism is evident in many of its classical masterpieces, such as the stone carvings at Mahabalipuram [79].

74 Woman worshipping a sacred *pipal* tree.
75 Snake-stones. Bangalore, age unknown.
76 *Yakshi*. Bharhut, 2nd century BC.
77 Aiyannar village guardians. Tamil Nadu, age unknown.
78 Rickshaw drivers' shrine to local spirits. Madurai, age unknown.
79 The Descent of the Ganges. Mahabalipuram, 7th century.

78

79

80

81

82

The Temple as the Meeting Place of Men and Gods

The temple is the place where the gods most readily descend to earth. The texts state that a temple must be built on a site both ritually orientated and beautiful – preferably near trees and fresh water – and that the ground must first be consecrated by purificatory rites performed at the correct astrological moment. Temples are generally built in stone, said to be a hundred times more meritorious for the builder than impermanent constructions of wood.

The temple is a synoptic image, uniting several symbols. In its classical form, it is the cosmic pillar linking heaven and earth, the stable *axis mundi* around which the ever-moving world revolves. Simultaneously it is Mount Meru, the many-layered cosmic mountain [80] standing at the centre of the universe, and in a more general sense the Himalayas, on whose slopes the gods, especially Shiva, reside.

The proliferation of images was a gradual process in the development of Hinduism. In Bali [81], where a very pure form of the religion has been preserved, the shrine usually consists of empty thrones onto which the deities descend when invoked with the appropriate chants, rituals and offerings. As time progressed, increasingly elaborate temples became

veritable microcosms of the universe, beginning at the base with the animal kingdom, and working up through the human to the divine levels [82]. Patrons and builders were sometimes represented, particularly if the temple had been founded to commemorate a victorious battle or campaign [83].

While the soaring exterior of the temple-mountain alludes to the transcendence of the divine, the cave-like interior, conducive to introversion, refers to its immanence [84]. The temple's prime function is not to accommodate a congregation, but to provide a *mandir* ('reception hall') for the deities and a place where the individual comes into contact with these divine energies. Around the holy of holies (*garbha griha* = 'womb house') hover images of subsidiary deities and protectors against negative forces.

80 Rajarajeshvara Temple. Tanjore, 11th century.
81 Pura Bukit Sari Temple. Bali, 17th century.
82 Kandariya Mahadeva Temple. Khajuraho, 11th century.
83 Shri Rangannatha Temple. Shrirangam, 17th century.
84 Meenakshi Temple. Madurai, 17th century.

84

83

Heroes and Heroines

India continues to have a large body of exemplary role-models drawn from ancient times. These are celebrated not only in the epics such as the *Mahabharata* and the *Ramayana* but in the vast body of folk songs and stories which even today serves as entertainment and education for many of the rural people. Such stories have always been passed on both by professional story-tellers and by god-intoxicated saints, many of whom were themselves poets.

Manikka Vachaka [85] was one of the *nayanars*, Shaivite saints whose lyrical Tamil poems inspired a social revolution in medieval India, teaching against the restrictions of caste and the corruption of the rich and powerful. Narada [87], who inspired Valmiki to pen the *Ramayana*, appears in many Puranic stories. He invented the *vina* and is the leader of the heavenly musicians (*gandharvas*). Arjuna [88], hero of the *Mahabharata*, is the archetypal warrior, here shown wearing princely crown, jewelry, waistcloth and pattens. One female role-model is the lovely Uma ('Peace of the Night') [89] who, as the Goddess in her marriage to Shiva, is the archetype of domestic harmony.

The Hindu tradition of enlightened beings as cultural heroes is almost inconceivable in the West. Two historical examples are the custodians of Vedic wisdom Shukadeva [86] and Adi Shankara [90] (who lived in the 8th century). In this century, two of the most renowned saints became spontaneously enlightened in their late teens, having followed no formal spiritual path (*sadhana*) and no particular teacher. Ananda Mayi Ma [91] came from a simple Bengali village family, and Ramana Maharshi [92] lived all his life in a relatively isolated part of Tamil Nadu. Yet they inspired millions both in India and abroad, and continue to do so.

85 Manikka Vachaka. South India, 14th century.
86 The sage Shukadeva instructing King Savikshit. Kishangarh school, c. 1760.
87 Narada. Madras, early 19th century.
88 Arjuna. South India, 19th century.
89 Uma preparing for her wedding with Shiva. Mattancheri Palace, Cochin, early 17th century.
90 Adi Shankara. Modern.
91 Shri Ananda Mayi Ma.
92 Bhagwan Shri Ramana Maharshi.

85

86

87

88

89

90

91

92

The Evolving Cosmos

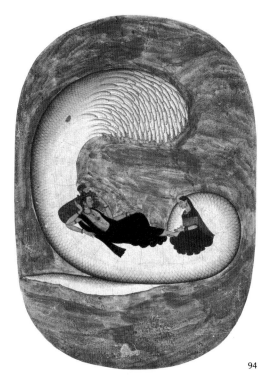

93

94

95

Creation begins with the golden Egg of Brahman [93], emerging from the depths of the ocean of unbounded Consciousness. From the pure potential of this seed emerge all the dualities that compose life – spirit and matter, male and female, light and dark – here [94] symbolized by Vishnu Narayana and his consort Lakshmi, seated on the limitless potential of the thousand-headed serpent 'Unending'. In the microcosm, the same process takes place each time the fertilized egg begins the duplication of cells that lead to the creation of a new form.

At the causal level, the prior nature of Consciousness, symbolized as Shiva, was established when Shiva appeared in an infinite *lingam* of fire [95]. He invited his rivals Brahma and Vishnu to discover the limits of the flaming pillar. Brahma, as a goose, flew into the air; Vishnu, as a boar, burrowed down into the earth. While Vishnu admitted he could not find the end, Brahma claimed to have done so, for which lie he lost the right to be worshipped, and Shiva's supremacy was demonstrated.

A complementary description has the universe created out of sound; the primordial vibration OM [96] containing all others in seed form. Sound structures the abstract or subtle bodies (*yantra*) of all forms, and by sound they can be moved into a higher vibrational frequency, i.e. spiritualized. The subtle body of the universe is represented by the Shri Yantra [97], which depicts the materialization of existence from Consciousness, moving from the abstract two-dimensional to the concrete three-dimensional image [98].

On the human level, the subtle body is the network of invisible conduits through which the life-energy circulates in the nervous system [99]. These join at seven principal nodes (*chakras* or 'lotuses'). Spiritual evolution reverses the downward flow of manifesting Consciousness, and proceeds by releasing the blocks that inhibit the circulation of life-energy in the subtle body. This frees individual awareness from being bound to the lower, material *chakras*, and allows it to rise through the higher, spiritual ones, eventually to reunite with its cosmic source. In yoga this ascent is known as 'the *lingam* of fire'.

93 The Egg of Brahman. Varanasi, age unknown.
94 Vishnu Narayana and Lakshmi. Guler school, c. 1760.
95 Shiva as the *lingam* of fire. Rajasthan, 18th century.
96 OM, the primordial vibration. Rajasthan, 19th century.
97 Shri Yantra. Rajasthan, 18th century.
98 Shri Yantra. 18th century.
99 The subtle body. Rajasthan, 18th century.

96

97

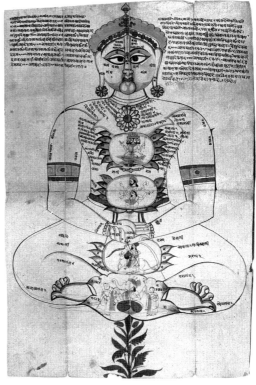

98

95

99

FURTHER READING

Baumer, B. (ed.), *Rupa Pratirupa*, New Delhi 1982.

Blurton, Richard T., *Hindu Art*, London 1992.

Boner, A., *Principles of Composition in Hindu Sculpture*, Leiden 1962.

——, *Vastu Sutra Upanishad*, Delhi 1982.

Burckhardt, T., *Sacred Art East and West*, Bedfont 1976.

Coomaraswamy, A., *The Transformation of Nature in Art*, New Delhi 1974.

Danielou, A., *Hindu Polytheism*, New York 1964.

——, *Shiva and Dionysius*, London 1982.

Harle, J. C., *The Art and Architecture of the Indian Sub-continent*, Harmondsworth 1986.

Hayward Gallery, London, *In the Image of Man*, London 1982.

Kramrisch, S., *Manifestations of Shiva*, Philadelphia 1981.

——, *The Presence of Shiva*, Princeton 1981.

——, *Exploring India's Sacred Art*, Philadelphia 1983.

Michell, G. (ed.), *Living Wood*, Bombay 1992.

Mitter, P., *Much Maligned Monsters*, Chicago 1992.

Mookerjee, A., and Khanna, M., *The Tantric Way*, London 1977.

Sahi, J., *The Child and the Serpent*, Harmondsworth 1990.

Williams, J. (ed.), *Kaladarshana*, New Delhi 1981.

Zimmer, H., *The Art of Indian Asia*, Princeton 1960.

——, *Myths and Symbols in Indian Art*, Princeton 1971.

——, *Artistic Form and Yoga in Sacred Images of India*, Princeton 1990.

ACKNOWLEDGMENTS

Figures in roman type refer to page numbers. Figures in *italic* type refer to illustrations in the themes section between pp. 66 and 95. The following abbreviations are used: *a* above, *b* below, *l* left, *r* right:

Boston: Courtesy, Museum of Fine Arts, Ross Collection *39*; Photo Raymond Burnier *42r*, *58al*, *59a*; Calcutta: Indian Museum *42l*, 76; Delhi: Indian Museum. Photo Louis Frédéric *10*; Photo Eliot Elisofon *58*; Photo Hinz, Basel 24; Photo Martin Hürlimann *9*, *56*; Hyderabad State: Alampur Museum *20*; Kansas City, Missouri: Collection of William Rockhill Nelson Gallery of Art, Atkins Museum of Fine Arts 66; Photo Richard Lannoy *36b*, 38, 43, 47, 54–55, *42*, *59*, *60*, *61*, *68*, *71*, *73*, *74*, *84*, *89*, *91*; Leiden: Rijksmuseum voor Leiden *44*; London: British Library 40–41; British Museum 4, 11, *11*, *25*, *26*, *30*, *48*, *54*, *85*; India Office Library *28br*, 35, *13*; By courtesy of the Board of Trustees of the Victoria & Albert Museum 13, 14, 20, *4*, *15*, *16*, *23*, *31*, *32*, *34*, *36*, *37*, *46*, *47*, *52*, *57*, *86–8*; Madras: Government Museum *12*; Photo Frank Monaco 46, 50, 51, 62, 63, 64; Ajit Mookerjee Collection 8, 21, 22, 30, 34, *8*, *41*, *67*, *69*, *70*, *93*, *95–99*; New Delhi: Department of Archaeology, Government of India *80*; New York: The Metropolitan Museum of Art (Eggleston Fund, 1927, 27.79) *14*; Oxford: Ashmolean Museum 21, 27, 28, 35; Paris: Musée Guimet *2*, *3*, *38*, *51*, (photo Werner Forman) *59b*; Photo Josephine Powell *49*, *64*, *79*; Private Collection 17, *40*, *94*; Photo Pierre Rambach *55*; Sarnath: Archaeology Museum *33*; Seattle Art Museum 65; Photo Alistair Shearer front cover, 48, 49, *58ar*, *58b*, *5*, *7*, *17*, *29*, *43*, *45*, *50*, *53*, *62*, *63*, *65*, *72*, *75*, *77*, *78*, *81*, *82*, *83*, *92*; Photo courtesy Alistair Shearer *17*, *92*; Udayagiri, Madhya Bharat *39*; Photo Paul Wakefield 33, 37, 52, 53, 56–57; Washington: Freer Gallery of Art, Smithsonian Institution 24; Photo Henry Wilson *36a*, *44*, *45*, *60–61a*, *61b*; Zurich: Museum Rietberg, Collection Von der Heydt 6. Figs. 1–6 are based on A. Boner, *Vastu Sutra Upanishad*.